Quizzes exert a fascination over anyone with a lively and inquiring mind. This book includes hundreds of fascinating questions, many with unexpected answers, and should intrigue, entertain and stimulate the whole family.

What was the name of Alexander the Great's horse? . . . Why is a boudoir so called? You might remember, or you could have to search out the answers, but in either case you will have great fun trying to beat the question masters.

Quintessential Quizzes is compiled by Norman Hickman, a native New Yorker, with adaptations by Ian Gillies, winner of the 'Top Brain' award of the BBC's 'Brain of Britain' competition. It is introduced by Irene Thomas, herself a former Brain of Britain and regular member of the Round Britain Quiz team. Good luck in your attempts to outwit them!

D1797437

QUINTESSENTIAL QUIZZES

A Collection of Curious Words, Derivations, Literary Allusions, and Little-Known Oddities of Fact and Fiction

NORMAN G. HICKMAN

Adapted by Ian Gillies

Foreword by Irene Thomas

London
UNWIN PAPERBACKS
Boston   Sydney

First published in Great Britain by Unwin Paperbacks 1982

Unwin® Paperbacks
40 Museum Street, London WC1A 1LU, UK

Unwin Paperbacks
Park Lane, Hemel Hempstead, Herts HP2 4TE, UK

George Allen & Unwin Australia Pty Ltd.
8 Napier Street, North Sydney, NSW 2060, Australia

© Norman G. Hickman, 1979, 1982
English revisions©Ian Gillies, 1982

British Library Cataloguing in Publication Data

Hickman, Norman G.
 Quintessential quizzes.
1. Questions and answers
I. Title   II. Gillies, Ian
793.73   AG195

ISBN 0-04-793050-0

Set in 9 on 10 point Univers Medium
by V & M Graphics Ltd, Aylesbury, Bucks
and printed in Great Britain
by The Anchor Press Ltd, Tiptree, Essex

FOREWORD

Ever since the day when Oedipus solved the riddle of the Spinx, quizzes have fascinated everyone who has a lively and inquiring mind.

This book contains hundreds of intriguing questions, and some unusual answers which may cause many family arguments and much searching in reference-books to confirm half-remembered facts . . . like 'What was the name of Alexander the Great's horse?' . . . 'Why is a boudoir so called?' . . . or: 'Who wrote the words and music for "Stardust"?'. One of the categories I find most interesting is the one titled 'Who said it first?' . . . it's full of things I *thought* I knew!

It's all good, clean fun, and has been admirably 'translated from the American' by Ian Gillies, who is an expert question-setter himself, besides being 'Top Brain' in the BBC's 'Brain of Britain' contest – a very rare and hard-won honour.

Irene Thomas

PUBLISHER'S NOTE

This book is based upon the one volume *The Quintessential Quiz Book* first published in the United States of America. It has been anglicised by Ian Gillies for publication in two books. Many of the original questions are retained and the publishers acknowledge with thanks all those individuals who helped Norman Hickman in compiling his book.

Thanks are due for permission to reprint from the following copyright material:

Belloc, Hilaire, 'On His Books', *Sonnets and Verse* (London: Gerald Duckworth & Co. Ltd.). Reprinted by permission of A. D. Peters & Co. Ltd., London.

Churchill, Winston S., from *Painting as a Pastime* (London: Ernest Benn Ltd.). Reprinted by permission of Ernest Benn Ltd.

Housman, A. E., 'When I Was One and Twenty' and 'A Shropshire Lad', from authorised editions of *The Collected Poems of A. E. Housman* (New York: Holt, Rinehart & Winston, 1939, 1940, 1965. Copyright 1967–68 by Robert E. Symons). Reprinted by permission of Holt, Rinehart & Winston.

Nash, Ogden. 'The Pig', 'The Turtle', *Verses From 1929 On* (New York: Little, Brown & Co., 1933, 1940, 1930). Reprinted by permission of Little, Brown & Co.

Schickele, Peter. *The Definitive Biography of P. D. Q. Bach* (London: Cassell Ltd., 1978). Reprinted by permission of Cassell Ltd.

Thurber, James. Reprinted by permission of Mrs James Thurber for one cartoon caption copyright 1943 by James Thurber. Renewed 1971. From *Men, Women and Dogs*, published by Harcourt Brace Jovanovich. Originally printed in *The New Yorker*.

CONTENTS

BEGINNINGS

1. What is the first verse in the Bible?
2. Which famous play begins with this line?
   'If music be the food of love, play on.'
3. Where do they remember the First Fleet every 26 January?
4. Who wrote both the words and the music of 'Begin the Beguine'?
5. Which well-known novel starts as follows?
   'It was the best of times, it was the worst of times, it was the age of wisdom, it was the age of foolishness, it was the epoch of belief, it was the epoch of incredulity, it was the season of Light, it was the season of Darkness, it was the spring of hope, it was the winter of despair...'
6. In which play is 'the beginning of fairies' explained?
7. 'Last night I dreamt I went to Manderley again' is the opening sentence of which novel?
8. According to the Bible, what is 'the beginning of wisdom'?
9. Who wrote the following lines?
   'From quiet homes and first beginning,
     Out to the undiscovered ends,
   There's nothing worth the wear of winning,
     But laughter and the love of friends.'
10. On what turning point in World War II did a nation's leader speak as follows?
    'Now this is not the end. It is not even the beginning of the end. But it is, perhaps, the end of the beginning.'

BEGINNINGS

1. 'In the beginning God created the heaven and the earth.'
   – Genesis 1:1.
2. *Twelfth Night*, by William Shakespeare.
3. In Australia. The First Fleet took the first settlers from Britain, and on 26 January 1788 Captain Arthur Phillip, who commanded it, took formal possession of the entire eastern half of the continent. The 26 January is now Australia Day.
4. Cole Porter.
5. *A Tale of Two Cities*, by Charles Dickens.
6. *Peter Pan*, by Sir James Barrie. 'When the first baby laughed for the first time, the laugh broke into a thousand pieces and they all went skipping about, and that was the beginning of fairies.'
7. *Rebecca*, by Daphne du Maurier.
8. 'The fear of the Lord'. – Psalm 111:10.
9. Hilaire Belloc, 'Dedicatory Ode'.
10. Winston Churchill, in a speech at the Mansion House in London, November 1942, following the decisive British victory at El Alamein in World War II.

ACRONYMS

An acronym is a word formed from the initial letters of a name or by combining initial letters or parts of a series of words. How many of the following can you 'translate'?

1. RADAR
2. SCUBA
3. FLAK
4. QANTAS
5. LASER
6. GESTAPO
7. IATA
8. ERNIE
9. SWALK
10. FASGROLIA

ACRONYMS

1. **R**adio **D**etection **A**nd **R**anging
2. **S**elf-**C**ontained **U**nderwater **B**reathing **A**pparatus
3. **F**lieger **A**bwehr **K**anone (aircraft defence gun)
4. **Q**ueensland **A**nd **N**orthern **T**erritory **A**erial **S**ervices
5. **L**ight **A**mplification by **S**timulated **E**mission of **R**adiation
6. **G**eheime **S**taatspolizei (Secret State Police)
7. **I**nternational **A**ir **T**ransport **A**ssociation
8. **E**lectronic **R**andom **N**umber **I**ndicator **E**quipment
9. **S**ealed **W**ith **A** **L**oving **K**iss
10. **F**ast **Gro**wing **L**anguage of **I**nitials and **A**cronyms

AMERICAN LITERATURE

1. Which American classic is subtitled *Life in the Woods*?
2. What was the derivation of Samuel Langhorne Clemens's pen-name Mark Twain?
3. Who wrote 'The Legend of Sleepy Hollow' and 'Rip Van Winkle'?
4. Who offered this bit of literary criticism? What is the name of Barnaby Rudge's raven?
    'There comes Poe, with his raven, like Barnaby Rudge,
    Three-fifths of him genius and two-fifths sheer fudge.'
5. What author lived from 1898 until his death in 1916 at Lamb House, Rye, in Sussex?
6. In Fitzgerald's *The Great Gatsby*, where did Jay Gatsby give his fabulous parties?
7. Which famous fictional heroine was married to Charles Hamilton and Frank Kennedy?
8. Who is reputed to have directed that ten per cent of her ashes be sent to her agent?
9. In *The Gift of the Magi*, by O. Henry, what gifts were exchanged?
10. Who wrote these lines?
    'There is no Frigate like a Book
    To take us Lands away
    Nor any Coursers like a Page
    Of prancing Poetry'

AMERICAN LITERATURE

1. *Walden*, by Henry David Thoreau.
2. 'Mark Twainl', meaning two fathoms, was the leadsman's cry Clemens had heard many times during his years as a steamboat pilot on the Mississippi.
3. Washington Irving.
4. James Russell Lowell in 'A Fable for Critics'. The name of Barnaby Rudge's raven is Grip.
5. Henry James. He became a British subject in 1915, some six months before he died.
6. At his mansion in West Egg, Long Island, outside New York. West Egg is a fictitious name, but the location corresponds to Sands Point or Great Neck.
7. Scarlett O'Hara in Margaret Mitchell's *Gone With The Wind.*
8. Dorothy Parker.
9. Jim sold his watch to buy his wife, Delia, a pair of tortoise-shell combs for her long, beautiful hair, while Delia sold her hair to buy Jim a platinum fob chain for his watch.
10. Emily Dickinson, No. 1263 (*The Complete Poems*).

THE ANCIENT WORLD

1. Can you name five of the Seven Wonders of the ancient world?
2. Where were the Pillars of Hercules?
3. Explain the origin of the suffix '-chester' in place names such as Rochester and Winchester.
4. Where did the Romans have their capital when they first occupied Britain?
5. What to the Greeks and Romans was Thule?
6. Why might we consider Naples a new city?
7. The little yellow finch known as the canary takes its name from the Canary Islands, where these birds abound, but to whom do the islands owe their name?
8. Which Aegean island's destruction by a volcanic eruption around 1500 BC is believed to have inspired the legend of Atlantis?
9. The ancient Greeks considered themselves descended from a mythical Hellen and called their land Hellas. How did the name Greece come about?
10. The beginning of what is now Paris was an island in the Seine which the Romans called Lutetia. How did the name Paris come into being?

THE ANCIENT WORLD

1. The Great Pyramid of Cheops (Egypt), the Hanging Gardens of Babylon (Iraq), the Tomb of King Mausolus at Halicarnassus (Turkey), the Temple of Artemis at Ephesus (Turkey), the Colossus of Rhodes (the Isle of Rhodes in the Aegean), the Statue of Zeus at Olympia (Greece), and the lighthouse on the Isle of Pharos (off Alexandria, Egypt).

2. At the eastern entrance to the Strait of Gibraltar. One pillar was Calpe, the Rock of Gibraltar, and the other Mount Abyla in North Africa.

3. It derives from the Old English *ceaster* or *caester*, meaning city or (Roman) town, and itself borrowed from the Latin *castra*, camp. The suffix was added to the Celtic name, or part of it; Winchester having been Venta and Rochester Durobrivae.

4. Camulodunum, on the site of present-day Colchester.

5. An island which was the most northerly point of the known world. It may have been Iceland, or Shetland, or Scandinavia.

6. Because when the Greeks first settled there, they called it *Neapolis*, meaning 'new town'. This later became *Napoli*, and Naples in English.

7. To the Romans who, when they first landed there, were so amazed at the number of wild dogs that they named the land *canaria insula*, the island of the dogs.

8. The Greek island of Thira, Thera or Santorin.

9. The *Graikoi* or, in Latin, *Graeci*, were the first Hellenic tribe the Romans encountered in the western part of Hellas. They proceeded to use this tribal name for the whole country so that now the land is known as Greece.

10. Since the tribe that inhabited the island were known to the Romans as the Parisii, they called the settlement *Lutetia Parisiorum*, or Lutetia of the Parisians. Over the years the shortened name Paris was adopted for the city.

ANIMALS

1. The word *animal* is ultimately derived from the Latin word *anima*, which means what?
2. Who wrote a description of a farm on which men and pigs become indistinguishable?
3. A camelopard is an archaic term for what?
4. Can you give the common Swahili word for lion?
5. *Nanook*, in the Eskimo tongue, is what?
6. What kind of animal was Bagheera, and whom did he teach?
7. Give the correct term for the American buffalo.
8. What does a pangolin eat?
9. The skin of what animal is called Hudson Seal by furriers?
10. Can you name the author of the following?
    'The pig, if I am not mistaken
    Supplies us sausage, ham and bacon.
    Let others say his heart is big,
    I call it stupid of the pig.'

ANIMALS

1. Breath.
2. George Orwell, in *Animal Farm*.
3. A giraffe.
4. *Simba*.
5. A polar bear.
6. A black panther. Mowgli. (*The Jungle Books*, by Rudyard Kipling.)
7. The American bison.
8. Termites, ants and other insects.
9. The muskrat.
10. Ogden Nash, 'The Pig', from *Happy Days*.

ASTROLOGY

1. Give the first and last signs of the zodiac, and the number of degrees in each sign. What is considered to be New Year's Day in astrology?
2. Why is the word *zodiac* a misnomer?
3. Which astronomer put astrology into a temporary eclipse?
4. In addition to the signs, the zodiac is divided into what the ancients considered the four great elements of air, fire, water, and earth. Do you know the astrological triplicities of these elements?
5. Who observed that 'The fault . . . is not in our stars, But in ourselves, that we are underlings'?
6. Which is usually considered to be the highest and most developed mental sign in the zodiac?
7. What is meant by the cusps?
8. Which sign represents the sexual or procreative element of man?
9. To cast your own horoscope is really quite simple. All you need is what?
10. Which group, in 1975, issued a statement saying that astrology has no basis in fact and contributes dangerously to 'the cult of irrationalism and obscurantism'?

ASTROLOGY

1. Aries and Pisces. Thirty degrees. 21 March.
2. Zodiac means 'ring of animals', yet there are four human signs represented – Gemini the Twins, Virgo the Virgin, Sagittarius the Archer, and Aquarius the Water Bearer – and one object, Libra the Scales.
3. Nicholas Copernicus, the sixteenth-century Polish astronomer who proved that the sun was the centre of our system and that the earth was one of the planets that revolved around it. Before this, astrologers had based their calculations on the Ptolemaic System, which held that the earth was the centre, with the sun revolving around it. Understandably, astrology fell into great disfavour following Copernicus's discovery.
4. Air: Gemini, Libra, and Aquarius. Fire: Aries, Leo, and Sagittarius. Water: Cancer, Scorpio, and Pisces. Earth: Taurus, Virgo, and Capricorn.
5. Cassius in Shakespeare's *Julius Caesar*.
6. Aquarius, the symbol of which is waves, which represent not water, as is generally thought, but electricity or vibration. These waves are also referred to as parallel lines of force.
7. Cusps (Latin *cuspis*, point) are the transitional first and last parts of a house or sign.
8. Scorpio.
9. To cast your own horoscope you will need the following: a) a blank horoscope map, b) your date, hour, and place of birth, c) an atlas, to determine the exact latitude and longitude of your birthplace, d) an ephemeris, a book giving the places of the planets on your birthday, e) a table of houses, giving the position and degrees of the signs, f) an aspect finder, giving the configuration of the stars and planets in relation to one another and to you, g) a book with interpretations of aspects and planetary positions.
   To go through all this, you just have to believe in astrology.
10. Eighteen Nobel laureates.

BATHROOM AND BOUDOIR

1. The word *boudoir* comes from the French word *bouder*, which means what?
2. What do women use that means in Latin 'to float through the air like smoke'?
3. If you were walking on the streets of old Edinburgh, why would the cry of 'gardy-loo' be alarming?
4. Of what is castile soap supposed to be made?
5. Which of the constellations does legend say is the shorn locks of a queen of Egypt?
6. Which mistress of Louis XV of France gave her name to a distinctive type of hair arrangement and how has this now cropped even closer to a head of state?
7. What is kohl, and for what is it used in Moslem and Asian countries?
8. What was Sir John Harrington's contribution to bathroom efficiency?
9. Who, in the Old Testament, 'painted her face, and tired her head, and looked out at a window'?
10. Which is the stronger, toilet water or cologne?

BATHROOM AND BOUDOIR

1. To sulk, or to pout. The boudoir, then, is literally the sulking or pouting room.
2. Perfume, from the Latin *per-*, meaning through, and *fumus*, meaning smoke.
3. It was a cry, taken from the French, that slops were being emptied out of an upstairs window, the 'loo' being a corruption of the French *l'eau*, meaning water.
4. Olive oil.
5. Coma Berenices, Berenice's Hair.
6. Madame de Pompadour, a modified version of whose hairdo is worn by Ronald W. Reagan.
7. A preparation, made from powdered antimony, used by women to darken the edges of the eyelids.
8. He invented the flush lavatory, installing one for Queen Elizabeth I in her palace at Richmond, Surrey.
9. Jezebel. – 2 Kings 9:30.
10. Toilet water.

BRITISH HISTORY

1. Why was Ethelred the Unready not ready?
2. In 1066 William the Conqueror defeated Harold at the Battle of Hastings. From what battle had Harold just come?
3. In 900 years England has had eight of two of them, and two of two of them. What are they?
4. When James I became King of England in 1603 why was he already an old king?
5. Which noble houses were involved in the 'Wars of the Roses'?
6. The Earl of Rochester wrote the following on the bedchamber door of which ruler?

   'Here lies our sovereign lord the king
   Whose promise none relies on;
   He never said a foolish thing,
   Nor ever did a wise one.'

   What was the king's amiable response to this attack?
7. Why would the phrase, 'New plan to study history wisely', be helpful to a student of British history?
8. What is missing from the following list: Blenheim, Oudenarde, Malplaquet?
9. During World War I why could the British forces on the Western Front be said to have switched from vermouth to whisky?
10. Can you name the four countries which gained their independence from Britain in 1947 and 1948? Which of them did not become a member of the Commonwealth?

BRITISH HISTORY

1. He was not; he was all too ready to act. The epithet does not mean 'unprepared', but derives from the Old English *unraed*, meaning 'without counsel'. Ethelred the Unready was so called because he refused to take advice.
2. From the battle of Stamford Bridge where he had routed the forces of Harold III of Norway. His defeat at Hastings has been attributed in part to the general exhaustion of his troops after the long march south.
3. Kings. There have been eight Edwards and eight Henrys, but only two Jameses and two Charleses.
4. He was already James VI of Scotland.
5. The House of York, whose badge was a white rose, fought the House of Lancaster, whose badge was a red rose, during the fifteenth century.
6. Charles II, who replied: 'This is very true, for my words are my own, and my actions are my ministers'.'
7. Because the initial letter of each word indicates the principal royal houses: Norman, Plantagenet, Tudor, Stuart, Hanover, Windsor.
8. Ramillies. These are the four great victories credited to the Duke of Marlborough in the War of the Spanish Succession.
9. Because General Haig replaced Field Marshal French as commander-in-chief of the British Expeditionary Force in 1915.
10. India, Pakistan, Burma, and Ceylon. Burma did not join the Commonwealth.

BRITISH ROYALTY AND PEERAGE

1. What is omitted from this list: Chester, Cornwall, Rothesay, Carrick, Renfrew, The Isles, Scotland?
2. Give in order of descending precedence, excluding royalty and clergy, the grades of the British peerage.
3. What is wrong with the legend about King Knut, otherwise known as Canute, taking his courtiers to the seashore to show he was so powerful that he could stop the tide from advancing?
4. What do the Dukedoms of Buccleuch, Grafton, Richmond, and St Albans have in common?
5. Where in England is the sovereign not permitted to enter?
6. Which First Lord of the Admiralty had an important group of islands named after him?
7. What was the original family name of the House of Windsor?
8. Many British military heroes who were created peers appended the locations of their most famous battles or campaigns to their names. Can you give the place names included in the titles of Field Marshals Kitchener, Alexander, and Montgomery?
9. In 1978 what happened to British royalty for the first time since 1540?
10. If a peer was convicted of murder while the death penalty was still in effect, what special privileges would he have?

BRITISH ROYALTY
AND PEERAGE

1. Wales. The list comprises the titles of Prince Charles, who is Earl of Chester, Duke of Cornwall, Duke of Rothesay, Earl of Carrick, Baron Renfrew, Lord of the Isles, Great Steward of Scotland, and, of course, Prince of Wales.
2. Duke, marquess, earl, viscount, and baron.
3. Just the opposite is true. Tired of the flattery of his court, Canute showed them he was powerless to stem the tide.
4. They derive from extra-marital affairs of Charles II with Lucy Walter; Barbara, Lady Castlemaine; Louise, Duchess of Portsmouth; and Nell Gwynn, respectively.
5. The House of Commons.
6. The fourth Earl of Sandwich, who had the Sandwich (now the Hawaiian) Islands named in his honour by Captain James Cook. It is probable that the Earl was responsible for the sandwich, which enabled him to eat without leaving the gaming table.
7. Wettin, which was the family name of Albert of Saxe-Coburg-Gotha, consort of Queen Victoria, was changed to Windsor by George V in 1917. Queen Elizabeth II, who married Philip Mountbatten, Duke of Edinburgh, decreed in 1952 that she and her children (except females who marry) shall be styled and known as the House and Family of Windsor.
8. Khartoum, Tunis, and Alamein.
9. A divorce, between Princess Margaret and Lord Snowdon. This was the first in the royal family since Henry VIII had his marriage to Anne of Cleves annulled. (George IV made an unsuccessful attempt, immediately after his accession to the throne in 1820, to divorce his long-estranged wife Caroline.)
10. He could choose to be hanged by a silken cord instead of a hempen rope. (Trial by one's peers in the House of Lords, in the case of treason and felony, was abolished by the Criminal Justice Act of 1948.)

BUILDINGS

1. A building owned by a triskaidekaphobiac would probably lack what?
2. Why might the Roman emperor Nero be considered to have made the word *palace* a common noun?
3. What is a hogan?
4. Whose official residence is the Palais Schaumburg?
5. Where is the largest residential complex for an individual in the world?
6. Who designed the first geodesic dome?
7. Do you know the name of the most famous 'temporary' structure in the world?
8. What was Versailles before it became a palace?
9. Of what famous building in England was this observation made: 'The dome of St Paul's must have come down . . . and pupped.'?
10. What are the three orders of classical Greek architecture?

BUILDINGS

1. A thirteenth floor, which would appear as the fourteenth. The long word means an abnormal fear of the number 13.
2. His residence was called the *palatium* because it stood on the Palatine Hill which probably derives its name from once having been palisaded. The word entered English as 'paleys' and later became 'palace'.
3. It is an earth-covered Navaho dwelling.
4. The Chancellor of the Federal Republic of Germany. The Palais Schaumburg is in Bonn.
5. The Vatican, in Rome.
6. Buckminster Fuller, the American architect and engineer.
7. The Eiffel Tower, which was built as an attraction for the Paris exposition of 1889 and named after its designer.
8. A hunting lodge.
9. The Royal Pavilion, also known as 'The Onion Patch', at Brighton. John Nash designed it for the Prince Regent in an ornate Eastern style featuring minarets and onion-domes. The comment was made by Sydney Smith.
10. Doric, Ionic, and Corinthian.

CHARACTERS IN LITERATURE

1. Who was 'willin''?
2. Natty Bumppo is the hero of which series of novels by whom?
3. Name the author of *Six Characters in Search of an Author*.
4. A picnic lunch of 'coldtonguecoldhamcoldbeefpickled-gherkinssaladfrenchrollscresssandwichespottedmeat-gingerbeerlemonadesodawater' was shared by whom?
5. Which writer named his hero after a well-known authority on the birds of the West Indies?
6. Who was the bride of Angel Clare?
7. Why does a certain character sport a price tag bearing the legend: 'In this style 10/6'?
8. In which novel is a leading character an American newspaper correspondent who has been emasculated?
9. Who was 'demned elusive'?
10. Where might you have found these colourful gentlemen: Harry the Horse, Franky Ferocious, Spanish John, Joey Uptown, Rope McGonnigle, Dancing Dan, Izzy Cheesecake, and Benny South Street?

CHARACTERS IN LITERATURE

1. Barkis, in Charles Dickens's *David Copperfield*, in which he sent a message to Clara Peggotty that 'Barkis is willin'.'
2. The *Leatherstocking Tales*, by James Fenimore Cooper. The title is derived from the nickname of the hero, so called because of his long deerskin stockings.
3. Luigi Pirandello.
4. The Water Rat and the Mole, in Kenneth Grahame's *The Wind in the Willows*.
5. Ian Fleming, in his James Bond stories.
6. Tess Durbeyfield, in *Tess of the D'Urbervilles*, by Thomas Hardy.
7. Because he was the Mad Hatter in Lewis Carroll's *Alice in Wonderland*. The price of the hat was ten shillings and sixpence.
8. *Fiesta – The Sun Also Rises*, Ernest Hemingway's first novel. The character was Jake Barnes.
9. The Scarlet Pimpernel, otherwise known as Sir Percy Blakeney, in a series of adventures about the French Revolution by Baroness Orczy (Mrs Montague Barstow).
   'We seek him here, we seek him there,
   Those Frenchies seek him everywhere.
   Is he in heaven? – Is he in hell?
   That demned elusive Pimpernel?'
10. Most probably in Mindy's, Damon Runyon's name for Lindy's Restaurant, a famous former Broadway landmark.

CHRISTMAS

1. Of which name is Santa Claus a contraction?
2. What part of Africa got its name because it was first sighted by Vasco da Gama on Christmas Day?
3. What was to happen on Christmas morning that made Beatrix Potter's Tailor of Gloucester so anxious to finish a coat?
4. Of where was 'good King Wenceslas' the ruler?
5. On what date does 'the Feast of Stephen' fall?
6. Is 'Xmas' a proper abbreviation for Christmas?
7. In Charles Dickens's *A Christmas Carol*, what was the full name of Ebenezer Scrooge's late partner?
8. Can you punctuate correctly this traditional Yuletide greeting?
    'God rest you merry gentlemen'.
9. Who was St Nicholas?
10. In which work do the following lines concerning the Christmas season appear?
    'It faded on the crowing of the cock.
    Some say that ever 'gainst that season comes
    Wherein our Saviour's birth is celebrated,
    The bird of dawning singeth all night long;
    And then, they say, no spirit can walk abroad;
    The nights are wholesome; then no planets strike,
    No fairy takes, nor witch hath power to charm,
    So hallow'd and so gracious is that time.'

CHRISTMAS

1. The Dutch *Sint Nikolaas* (Saint Nicholas). In the Netherlands and elsewhere the feast of St Nicholas is celebrated on 6 December, which is a children's holiday, when gifts are presented to them.
2. Natal, now a province of the Republic of South Africa.
3. The Mayor of Gloucester was to be married, and the coat was for him to wear.
4. Bohemia, which is now part of Czechoslovakia. Vaclav, as Wenceslas is called in Czech, was Duke of Bohemia in the early tenth century.
5. The 26 December. St Stephen was the first Christian martyr.
6. Yes, it goes back to Old English. (The Greek word for 'Christ' begins with the letter *chi*, or *x*.)
7. Jacob Marley.
8. 'God rest you merry, gentlemen'. The phrase 'rest you merry' goes back to the fifteenth century.
9. A fourth-century bishop of Myra, in Asia Minor. He is the patron saint of children, virgins, sailors, thieves, and pawnbrokers, as well as of Sicily, Greece, and Russia.
10. In the opening scene of Shakespeare's *Hamlet* when Marcellus, an officer of the guard, explains to Horatio the reason for the disappearance of the ghost of Hamlet's father, the dead King of Denmark.

CITIES AND TOWNS

1. Where would you find the Spanish Steps?
2. Give two former names of the city now known as Leningrad.
3. In which well-known play does the stage manager play an important role?
4. Which city lends its name to an accent, a car, a cloth, a colour, a dictionary, a Group, a marmalade, a Movement, and shoes?
5. Who was the author of the atheistic and despairing poem 'The City of Dreadful Night'?
6. The name of which city is used as a verb meaning 'to kidnap a person for compulsory service aboard a ship, especially after rendering him insensible'?
7. Which well-known magazine, according to its first editor, Harold Ross, was not 'edited for the old lady from Dubuque'?
8. What was the name of the fabulous 'City of Gold' which the early Spanish explorers sought in South America?
9. With which fictional city do you associate Babbitt in Sinclair Lewis's novel?
10. Can you name the new town in County Durham that is named after a miners' leader, and the one in Shropshire named after a Scottish civil engineer?

CITIES AND TOWNS

1. Rome.
2. St Petersburg and Petrograd.
3. *Our Town*, by Thornton Wilder.
4. Oxford.
5. James Thomson.
6. Shanghai. This was fairly common practice in the China trade, especially on ships sailing between San Francisco and Shanghai.
7. *The New Yorker*.
8. El Dorado. The legend of El Dorado, 'the gilded man', supposedly originated with the Chibcha Indians of Colombia who each year anointed a chieftain with gold. He then ceremoniously washed off the gold in a sacred lake into which offerings of emeralds and gold were dropped.
9. Zenith, a midwestern boom city.
10. Peterlee. Telford.

CLOTHES

1. What titled family gave its name to a sofa, an overcoat, and a cigarette?
2. What uniform, still in use, was designed by Michelangelo, or possibly by Raphael?
3. The most popular clothes in the Western World are known as jeans, denims, and Levi's. Do you know the origins of these words?
4. Who designed 'Gorgeous' Gussie Moran's lace panties for the Wimbledon tennis championships of 1949?
5. What were Cinderella's slippers made of?
6. Who described whom as 'The glass of fashion and the mould of form'?
7. Where would you expect to find an aglet?
8. How did the word 'suede', for leather with a soft napped surface, come into the English language?
9. What is the only piece of headgear to be named after a poem?
10. Who originated the fashion of leaving the bottom button of a waistcoat unbuttoned?

CLOTHES

1. The Chesterfield family.
2. That worn by the Swiss Guard at the Vatican.
3. Jeans and denims are anglicised versions of two cities where the cloth was first made, Genoa in Italy and Nîmes in southern France, respectively. Levi's owe their name to Levi Strauss, who, during the Gold Rush days in California, brought the coarse twilled material west with him to make tents and wagon covers for the miners. On finding they needed new trousers more than tents, he adapted his cloth to this purpose. The company bearing his name still exists.
4. Teddy Tinling.
5. Most likely of fur and not glass. It is believed that when Charles Perrault wrote down the Cinderella story in 1697, he mistook the old French word *vair*, meaning 'ermine', for *verre*, which means 'glass'.
6. Ophelia, speaking of Hamlet, in Act III, Scene 1 of Shakespeare's play.
7. At the end of your shoelace. An aglet is the metal sheath attached to the end of a lace to facilitate its passing through the eyelet holes. It derives from the diminutive of the Latin *acus*, needle.
8. From Sweden, which first exported this leather in the form of gloves. (French *gants de suède*, gloves of Sweden.)
9. The tam-o'-shanter, from Robert Burns's 'Tam o' Shanter'.
10. King Edward VII, either inadvertently or because of his expanding girth.

COLOURS

1. In the context of the above, what do you suppose Roy G Biv means?
2. What colour is named after a battle fought in 1859?
3. What are the ingredients of the drink known as Black Velvet?
4. Literature's Hester Prynne was condemned to wear what for life?
5. What is patently redundant about the acronym WASP, meaning 'White Anglo-Saxon Protestant'?
6. How did khaki originate as a shade for military uniforms?
7. What is the name of the 'rose-red city, half as old as time', and in which country is it located?
8. What was the proper name of the Prussian award nicknamed the Blue Max?
9. The subject of the popular song 'The object of my affection' can do what?
10. Who were known as the Black Friars?

COLOURS

1. The letters represent the range of colours in the spectrum: red, orange, yellow, green, blue, indigo, violet.
2. Magenta, the battle between the French and Sardinians, and the Austrians. The vivid purplish-red dye was discovered in the year of the battle, and was named for its bloodiness.
3. Champagne and stout.
4. A scarlet letter *A*, for adulteress. The novel, *The Scarlet Letter*, established Nathaniel Hawthorne's fame.
5. Have you ever heard of a black Anglo-Saxon?
6. The word 'khaki' comes from the Persian *khak*, meaning 'dust' or 'earth'. It was adopted by the British during the wars against the Sikhs in the mid-nineteenth century to replace the regulation red uniforms, which made too inviting a target.
7. Petra, in Jordan. The quotation is from the Newdigate Prize Poem, 'Petra', by John William Burgon.
8. The Military Order *Pour le Mérite*.
9. 'Change my complexion from white to rosy-red.'
10. The Dominicans, because of their black habits.

COUNTRIES

1. Which is the smallest country in the world?
2. In which country would you find Timbuktu, and for what was it famous?
3. Who said, 'Something is rotten in the state of Denmark'?
4. Which two countries joined in 1958 to form the United Arab Republic?
5. Which country was named after a circle on the earth?
6. In which country is Mount Aconagua, the highest peak in the Americas?
7. What are the former names of Belize, Benin, Botswana, Sri Lanka, and Zambia?
8. Is Iran a new name for Persia?
9. Which maritime country has the shortest coastline?
10. Which nation did not change the spelling of its name, but by official edict changed its pronunciation?

COUNTRIES

1. The smallest independent country in the world is the State of the Vatican City, with an area of 108.7 acres (44 hectares). It also has the smallest population and a zero birth rate.
2. Mali, in north-west Africa, near the head of the River Niger. Timbuktu, which was settled in 1087 by the Tuareg, was a centre of trade in gold, and its fame spread as far as Europe.
3. Marcellus, in Shakespeare's *Hamlet*.
4. Egypt and Syria. Syria withdrew in 1961, but Egypt continued to be known as the United Arab Republic until 1971.
5. The Republic of Ecuador, because it is crossed by a great circle on the earth, the equator, which in Spanish is *ecquador*.
6. Argentina, in the Andes. Aconagua is 22,834 feet (6,960 metres).
7. British Honduras, Dahomey, Bechuanaland, Ceylon and Northern Rhodesia.
8. No, the country has been known to the natives as Iran for centuries; foreigners called it Persia because they traded with the ancient kingdom of Pars (now the province of Fars) in the south-west part of Iran and bordering the Persian Gulf. The name Iran, which is derived from the same Indo-European root as 'Aryan', was officially adopted in 1935.
9. Monaco, with a coastline of about 3½ miles (5.6 km).
10. Kenya was formerly pronounced 'Keen-ya' but now is 'Kenya', to rhyme with the last name of its first leader, Jomo Kenyatta.

DANCE

1. What was the kordax?
2. In the early Renaissance, court dances became popular with established step patterns and rules. Can you name three out of seven of these dances? What form of music was developed from these?
3. In the field of dance, what notable event occurred at the court of Catherine de' Medici, Queen of Henry II of France?
4. Which king, who was a ballet dancer from the age of 13, founded the Royal Ballet Company in France?
5. With which countries are these dances associated: czardas, fandango, mazurka, tarantella, and the jig?
6. In 1909, who took to Paris a Russian company which dominated the world of dance? Name three of the leading choreographers and dancers from this company.
7. How did the famous American dancer Isadora Duncan meet her death in 1927?
8. What is the stage name of the dancer and choreographer whose real name is Edris Stannus?
9. Who specialised in dancing up and down stairs? Who made appearing to dance on the walls and ceiling famous?
10. In 1951, 1961, and 1968 which three choreographers won honorary Oscars for their work in films?

DANCE

1. It was an ancient Dionysian phallic dance performed in the nude.
2. Galliard, pavane, allemande, courante, saraband, gigue, and minuet. The sonata developed from these.
3. The first ballet which combined music, movement, and decoration was presented.
4. Louis XIV of France, in 1661.
5. Hungary, Spain, Poland, Italy and Ireland.
6. Sergei Diaghilev, Michel Fokine, Léonide Massine, Vaslav Nijinsky, Anna Pavlova, and George Balanchine.
7. Her neck was broken when the long scarf she was wearing became entangled in a rear wheel of her car while she was motoring in Nice.
8. Dame Ninette de Valois.
9. Bill 'Bojangles' Robinson. Fred Astaire.
10. Gene Kelly, for *An American in Paris*; Jerome Robbins, for *West Side Story*; and Onna White, for *Oliver!*

DOWNSTAIRS

1. What were the names of the cook and the butler of the Bellamy household in the television series *Upstairs, Downstairs*, and who played these parts?
2. Name the nanny who had a perfectly rolled umbrella with a parrot handle.
3. On Olympus, what were the duties of Hebe and Ganymede?
4. What is a 'tweeny'?
5. Identify Jean Passepartout.
6. Who played the part of Prissy, Scarlet O'Hara's highly-strung maid, in *Gone with the Wind*?
7. Who said, 'The cook was a good cook, as cooks go; and as cooks go she went'?
8. Describe the nurse of the Darling children in *Peter Pan*.
9. Can you name four works of fiction in English which showed that the valet or butler was invariably superior to his employer?
10. Who wrote, 'They also serve who only stand and wait'?

DOWNSTAIRS

1. Mrs Bridges and Mr Hudson, played by Angela Baddeley and Gordon Jackson.
2. Mary Poppins.
3. They were cupbearers to the gods.
4. A maid who assists both the cook and the housemaid; otherwise known as a betweenmaid, hence the term 'tweeny'.
5. Phileas Fogg's French servant who accompanied him on his trip around the world in eighty days, as described in the Jules Verne novel. (*Passepartout* in French means 'go everywhere' and also 'a master key'.)
6. Butterfly McQueen.
7. Saki (H. H. Munro), in *Reginald*.
8. She was a Newfoundland dog called Nana.
9. *Right Ho! Jeeves* (and others), by P. G. Wodehouse; *Ruggles of Red Gap*, by H. L. Wilson; *My Man Godfrey*, by Eric Hatch; and *The Admirable Crichton*, by Sir James M. Barrie.
10. John Milton, in the sonnet 'On His Blindness'.

EXPLORATION

1. Who is reported to have said, 'Along this track of pathless ocean I intend to steer'?
2. Who started the British Empire by establishing the first English possession outside Europe? Where and when was it?
3. Who was the first man to set foot on all the continents, excluding Antarctica?
4. Who discovered Florida, and why was it so named?
5. Of what nationality was the famous explorer John Cabot?
6. Who named the Pacific Ocean?
7. Sacajawea, an American Shoshoni Indian, accompanied which expedition as guide and the only woman in the party?
8. What was the name of Henry Hudson's ship?
9. Whose was the second party to reach the South Pole?
10. Who was the first to fly over the North Pole, and when was this flight made?

EXPLORATION

1. Christopher Columbus, the Admiral of the Ocean Sea, as Samuel Eliot Morison entitled his book about the great explorer.
2. Sir Humphrey Gilbert, the older half-brother of Sir Walter Raleigh, who established a colony at what is now St John's, Newfoundland, in 1583.
3. Captain James Cook.
4. Ponce de León, on Easter Sunday 1513. He named the land in honour of that day which in Spanish is *Pascua Florida*, or Flowery Easter.
5. He was born in Genoa, but later became a Venetian citizen. His real name was Giovanni Caboto.
6. Ferdinand Magellan, because of its peaceful appearance after he emerged from the Strait of Magellan.
7. The Lewis and Clark Expedition, which explored the territory of the Louisiana Purchase and the country beyond to the Pacific Ocean.
8. The *Half Moon*.
9. Captain Robert Falcon Scott, who failed in his race to the Pole with the Norwegian explorer, Roald Amundsen. Scott and his companions perished on the return trip to their base in March 1912.
10. Commander Richard E. Byrd, in the *Josephine Ford* on 9 May 1926. Amundsen, Ellsworth, and Nobile followed him three days later.

FAMILIAR MISQUOTATIONS

Can you complete these popular quotes correctly?
 1. 'All that .... is not gold.'
 2. 'To .... the lily.'
 3. '............ is the hobgoblin of little minds.'
 4. 'A little .... is a dangerous thing.'
 5. 'Alas! poor Yorick, ...'
 6. 'Imitation is the sincerest .... flattery.'
 7. '............ is a rose is a rose.'
 8. 'Music has charms to soothe a ....'
 9. 'Water, water everywhere .... drop to drink.'
10. '..........., my dear Watson.'

FAMILIAR MISQUOTATIONS

1. glisters (Shakespeare, *The Merchant of Venice*)
2. paint (Shakespeare, *King John*)
3. A foolish consistency (Emerson, *Essays* – 'Self-Reliance')
4. learning (Pope, *Essay on Criticism*)
5. I knew him, Horatio (Shakespeare, *Hamlet*)
6. of (Colton, *Lacon*)
7. Rose (Gertrude Stein, 'Sacred Emily')
8. savage breast (Congreve, *The Mourning Bride*)
9. nor any (Coleridge, *The Rime of the Ancient Mariner*)
10. If you answered 'Elementary', you are mistaken; in none of the Conan Doyle stories does Sherlock Holmes ever utter this phrase. In 'The Crooked Man', however, when Watson cries, 'Excellent!', Holmes replies, 'Elementary'.

FIRE

1. In what guise did God first talk to Moses?
2. Who was the author of the novel *Pale Fire*?
3. At sea the appearance of St Elmo's fire as fiery emanations from the tips of a ship's masts or spars is regarded as what?
4. On which island did the volcano of Mont Pelée erupt in 1902 with the loss of 40,000 lives?
5. Do you know the legend of how the great Chicago fire of 1871 was supposed to have started?
6. What causes most forest fires?
7. Who wrote *The Fire Next Time*, a series of essays on the feelings and attitudes of US blacks?
8. Why do fireflies light up?
9. Hephaestos and Vulcan have what in common?
10. Can you name the Poet Laureate who wrote the following?
    'Only stay quiet while the mind remembers
    The beauty of fire from the beauty of embers.'

FIRE

1. As a bush that 'burned with fire, and the bush was not consumed.'– Exodus 1:8.
2. Vladimir Nabokov.
3. A portent of bad weather.
4. Martinique.
5. Mrs O'Leary's cow kicked over a lantern. It later developed that a reporter made up the story to lend colour to his article on the fire.
6. Lightning.
7. James Baldwin.
8. As a form of sexual attraction. It is thought that the intensity and frequency of the flashes serve to identify males and females to one another.
9. They are respectively the Greek and Roman gods of fire and metalworking.
10. John Masefield, 'On Growing Old'.

FOOD

1. How did the ubiquitous hot dog get its name?
2. What does the dish known as chitterlings or chitlins consist of?
3. What is the probable derivation of mayonnaise?
4. Can you identify the edible fruit whose name is derived from the Nahuatl word for 'testicle'?
5. What is Bombay Duck, and when is it served?
6. Why is corned beef so named?
7. Which three ingredients are chiefly responsible for the distinctive flavour of Worcester Sauce?
8. Why is chowder named after a pot?
9. What is a sweetbread?
10. What is the name of a type of French eating establishment that came into the French language in 1814, during the post-Napoleonic occupation of Paris by the victorious troops of Czar Alexander I?

FOOD

1. From a cartoon of a dachshund inside an elongated bun – dachshund being a facetious symbol for things German in the early 1900s, when many people suspected the hot dog contained dog meat, or worse. This drawing was done by the popular sports cartoonist T. A. Dorgan who signed his work TAD.
2. The small intestines of pigs.
3. It is believed that mayonnaise was named to commemorate the capture of the city of Mahón, capital of Minorca in the Balearic Islands, by the Duc de Richelieu in 1756. After the supply of condiments had given out during the siege, his chief invented mayonnaise to supply the want.
4. The avocado, from the Nahuatl *ahuacatl* (in Spanish, *aguacate*).
5. It is a dried fish which is served as an accompaniment to curries.
6. Corned beef is beef preserved in salt, which at one time was in the form of pellets called corns.
7. Anchovies, soy and tamarinds.
8. In Brittany it was the custom for each fisherman to throw his catch into a community pot, or chaudière. The fame of this dish was such that it spread to Newfoundland and then to the east coast of the United States. The name of the pot was applied to its contents and restyled 'chowder'.
9. The thymus gland of an animal.
10. Bistro, from *bystro*, the Russian word for 'quickly'. It seems that certain sections of Paris were out of bounds to the Russians, and when the soldiers, disobeying the order, went into a tavern, they demanded fast service so that the patrols would not catch them.

FOREIGN TERMS
AND PHRASES

Give the English equivalent of the following:
1. *Vis-à-vis* (Fr.)
2. *Quid pro quo* (L.)
3. *Der Mensch ist was er isst* (Ger.)
4. *Cosi fan tutti* (It.)
5. *Amour-propre* (Fr.)
6. *Salaam aleikum* (Ar.)
7. *Dies Irae* (L.)
8. *Leibe kann viel, Geld kann alles* (Ger.)
9. *Soi-disant* (Fr.)
10. *Honi soit qui mal y pense* (Fr.)

FOREIGN TERMS
AND PHRASES

1. Face to face; opposite.
2. Something in return; a substitute.
3. Man is what he eats.
4. Thus do they all; that is the way of the world.
5. Self-esteem; vanity.
6. Peace be with you. (Moslem salutation.)
7. Day of wrath. (Hence, Day of Judgment: the title of a Latin hymn sung at solemn requiems.)
8. Love is mighty, but money is almighty.
9. Self-styled; pretended, would-be.
10. Shame on him who thinks evil of it. (This is the motto of the Most Noble Order of the Garter, the highest the Monarch can bestow.)

GOLF AND TENNIS

1. What is the full name of the international shrine of golf?
2. Which is more commonly played in this country, lawn tennis or court tennis?
3. What royal association may be attached to the word 'caddie'?
4. Why is the name of Major Walter C. Wingfield remembered?
5. Which three countries compete in the amateur biennial Walker Cup golf competition?
6. In which of Shakespeare's plays do you find tennis balls?
7. Can you explain how Joyce Wethered managed in 1927 to get two birdies in one hole?
8. Of the many derivations for the words 'tennis', 'set', and 'love', give those from the French.
9. In 1930 Bobby Jones became the first person to achieve a Grand Slam – that is, winning the US Amateur and Open, and the British Amateur and Open championships. For a Grand Slam today a player must win which four tournaments in a single year? Who was the first golfer to do this?
10. What two records did the Bear set at Wimbledon in 1980?

GOLF AND TENNIS

1. The Royal and Ancient Golf Club of St Andrews, Scotland, founded in 1754. It is a public course, municipally owned.
2. Lawn tennis, Court tennis, real or royal tennis (it was formerly a favourite of royalty) is played on a complex indoor court and dates back to medieval France, where it probably originated within the castle walls. It is the forerunner of most modern racquet games.
3. When Mary, Queen of Scots, returned to Scotland in 1561, she brought both her French court and a passion for golf. To retrieve her golf balls she used her young pages, who were called by the French word *cadet*. This later evolved into caddie.
4. He invented lawn tennis in 1873. It was first called *sphairistike*, meaning 'ball play' in Greek.
5. Great Britain and Ireland versus the United States.
6. *Henry V*.
7. Her drive struck a swallow.
8. 'Tennis' may be derived from the French *tenez*, an interjection approximating to 'Look here!' 'Set' probably comes from *sept*, dating from the days when it took seven, not six, games to make a set. For 'love' we have the French for the egg, *l'oeuf*, signifying zero.
9. The US Open, the US Masters, the PGA (USA), and the British Open. No golfer has ever done it.
10. Bjorn (which means Bear in Swedish) Borg won his fifth consecutive Wimbledon singles title, beating John McEnroe, and set another record of 35 consecutive match victories in Wimbledon play, exceeding Rod Laver's previous string of 31.

GOVERNMENT

1. What are the first ten amendments to the United States Constitution frequently called?
2. Can you name the two cities each of which is a separate Land, or State, of the Federal Republic of Germany?
3. How many republics are there in the USSR?
4. Which three countries became members of the European Community on 1 January 1973?
5. The symbol of a bundle of sticks tied around an axe gave its Latin name, *fasces*, to the political system of Fascism. Who first showed that whereas a single stick may be readily broken, this is not so when several are bound together in a bundle, and thus taught the lesson that 'Union gives strength'?
6. As applied to legislative bodies, what is meant by cloture?
7. Can you define pornocracy?
8. What do the initials SPQR signify?
9. Was the United Kingdom or the United States the first to adopt women's suffrage at the national level?
10. What has the term 'Salic law' come to mean?

GOVERNMENT

1. The Bill of Rights.
2. Hamburg and Bremen.
3. Fifteen.
4. The United Kingdom, the Republic of Ireland, and Denmark.
5. Aesop.
6. It is a parliamentary procedure for ending debate after which the matter under discussion is voted on immediately.
7. Prevalent in the Papal Court in the tenth century, pornocracy (from the Greek *porno*, prostitute, and *krates*, strength or power) means the influence of courtesans on the government.
8. *Senatus Populusque Romanus* – the Senate and the People of Rome.
9. The United Kingdom, in 1918 (at first to women over thirty). The United States followed in 1920.
10. A law believed to derive from the code of laws of the ancient Salic Franks, excluding females from succeeding, or transmitting the right to succeed to the throne. It was later used to bar women from the thrones of France and Spain.

HORSES

1. What are quarter horses?
2. Can you locate a horse's fetlock? His withers?
3. What is the name of the famous winged steed in Greek mythology?
4. Who rode these horses in films: Tony, Champion, and Scout?
5. Define the terms 'maiden' and 'yearling' as used in horse racing.
6. What is the present location of the four bronze horses which came originally from Constantinople and were taken by Napoleon?
7. Which British jockey rode the most winners during his career?
8. What are the five classics of the English flat-racing season?
9. Where would you find the line, 'A horse! a horse! my kingdom for a horse!'?
10. Can you name the steeds of Alexander the Great, Don Quixote, and the Duke of Wellington at Waterloo?

HORSES

1. They are a breed of strong saddle horses developed in the western United States and trained for races up to a quarter of a mile. The All-American Futurity, a series of elimination races for a purse exceeding one million dollars, the richest in the world, is held for quarter horses over 440 yards at Ruidosa Downs, New Mexico.
2. The fetlock is on the back side of the leg, above the hoof. The withers are the highest part of the back, located at the base of the neck and between the shoulder blades.
3. Pegasus.
4. Tom Mix, Gene Autry, and Tonto.
5. A maiden is generally a racehorse that has never won a race. A yearling is a thoroughbred racehorse that is one year old or has not completed its second year.
6. On a gallery over the main entrance to St Mark's Cathedral in Venice. Because of the pollution there, the horses have now been removed indoors and replaced by replicas.
7. Sir Gordon Richards, who rode 4,870 winners between 1912 and his retirement in 1954.
8. The Derby, the Two Thousand Guineas, the One Thousand Guineas, the Oaks, and the St Leger.
9. Shakespeare's *Richard III*, Act V, Scene 4.
10. Bucephalus, Rosinante, and Copenhagen.

HOUSE AND HOME

1. What famous song comes from the almost-forgotten opera *Clari, the Maid of Milan*, by Sir Henry Bishop, libretto by John Howard Payne?
2. What are lares and penates?
3. Where would an épergne be placed?
4. What is a canterbury?
5. Give the name of the fine glazed pottery made especially in France but originating in Italy.
6. For what is Grinling Gibbons famous?
7. Describe an oriel.
8. An ormolu object or ornamentation would have which colour?
9. Do you know the original function of the drawing room?
10. Can you define the following antique terms?
    a) Chinoiserie
    b) Bisque
    c) Grandmother
    d) Coquillage
    e) Niddy noddy
    f) Cachepot
    g) Bombé
    h) Farthingale
    i) Récamier
    j) Cabriole

HOUSE AND HOME

1. 'Home, Sweet Home.'
2. Esteemed household possessions, from the names of the Roman household gods.
3. At the centre of a table. It is a large silver or glass centrepiece.
4. A stand with divisions in it, for holding atlases, large books, music, etc.
5. Faience. The name derives from the French, short for (*vaiselle de*) *Faïence*, (vessel of) Faenza.
6. Fine woodcarving. He was a master woodcarver to the crown from the reign of Charles II to that of George I, and he was often employed by Sir Christopher Wren for architectural decoration.
7. It is a projecting bay window. The term is most usually applied to a bay window on an upper storey.
8. Golden. Ormolu is imitation gold and derives from the French *or moulu*, ground gold.
9. Originally it was the withdrawing room to which the ladies withdrew after dinner.
10. a) Imitating the Chinese
    b) Unglazed ceramic ware
    c) Small long-case clock
    d) Shell-like ornamentation
    e) Reel for winding yarn
    f) Ornamental container for a flowerpot
    g) Furniture with bulging front or sides
    h) Chair with a wide seat and no arms
    i) Couch or bed with head and feet scrolled outward
    j) A curved leg ending in an ornamental foot

INDIANS

1. How did the American Indians come into the western hemisphere?
2. What celebrated error in history led to the name 'Indian'?
3. Who did the Aztecs and their leader, whom we call Montezuma, believe Cortes and the Spaniards to be when they entered Mexico in 1519?
4. Whom did the Spaniards call Atahualpa?
5. By what name is the Apache leader Goyathlay better known – especially to paratroopers?
6. Describe wampum and tell its uses.
7. Were the Plains Indians always nomadic?
8. Can you identify Nokomis, Daughter of the Moon?
9. At the Battle of the Little Bighorn in 1876, who wiped out Custer and his men after they rashly attacked the largest Indian encampment in the Northwest?
10. Which are the three most populous Indian tribes in the United States?

INDIANS

1. It is generally believed that they came from Asia via the Bering Strait in a series of migrations. From Alaska they spread east and south.
2. Columbus, like other early explorers, thought he had reached the Indies of Asia. He therefore named the islands he visited the West Indies, and their inhabitants Indians.
3. The descendants of their great god Quetzalcoatl.
4. He was Atalabipa, the Inca of Peru and ruler of the Incan Empire when Pizarro and the Spaniards entered Peru in 1532. Atahualpa was executed, although he offered two rooms of gold and silver as ransom, which the Spanish accepted.
5. Geronimo. Goyathlay means 'One Who Yawns'. Paratroopers used to shout 'Geronimo!' as they jumped.
6. Wampum, small cylindrical beads made from polished shells, was used both as currency and jewellery.
7. No, not until the sixteenth century, when the Spanish brought horses to North America. Prior to that, since they lacked transportation, they generally stayed close to stream beds and lakes where game was plentiful.
8. Nokomis was Hiawatha's grandmother, in Longfellow's 'The Song of Hiawatha'.
9. Sioux and Cheyenne warriors, headed by the Sioux Chiefs Sitting Bull and Crazy Horse. Chief Crazy Horse actually led the attack on Custer and his men.
10. In descending order, they are Navaho, Cherokee, and Sioux.

ISLANDS

1. Which Mediterranean island was the seat of a high civilisation in pre-Hellenic times?
2. How did the Virgin Islands get their name?
3. What is the largest non-continental island mass in the world?
4. On which rainy island did the fanatical missionary Mr Davidson 'fall from grace' with the prostitute Sadie Thompson and as a consequence slit his throat?
5. Why are the Pacific islands of Juan Fernandez remembered?
6. Byron in *Don Juan* wrote that 'burning Sappho loved and sung'. With which island is she associated?
7. Name the four principal Channel Islands.
8. Can you locate the islands of Langerhans?
9. Islands seem to have played an important part in Napoleon's life. Name four with which he was intimately associated.
10. What is the most remote inhabited island in the world?

ISLANDS

1. Crete.
2. When Columbus discovered the Virgin Islands, he found them so numerous that he was reminded of the legend of St Ursula, the Virgin Martyr of Cologne, who, with her 11,000 virgin handmaidens, was murdered by Huns in the fourth century.
3. Greenland. (Australia is generally regarded as a continental land mass.)
4. Tutuila, one of the American Samoan islands, the principal town of which, Pago Pago, was the locale of W. Somerset Maugham's short story, 'Rain'.
5. After a quarrel with his captain in 1704, Alexander Selkirk, a Scottish sailor, asked to be put ashore here. He was picked up four years later, and his adventures suggested to Daniel Defoe the story of *Robinson Crusoe*, which appeared in 1719. One of the islands is now called Robinson Crusoe, and another Alejandro Selkirk. (Defoe's story was also influenced by Robert Knox, an English sailor who had written an account of nearly twenty years he had been forced to spend in Ceylon.)
6. The Greek island of Lesbos, from which the word 'lesbian' comes.
7. Jersey, Guernsey, Alderney, and Sark.
8. They are insulin-producing cells in the pancreas, the malfunction of which causes diabetes.
9. Corsica, where he was born; the Île de la Cité in Paris, where he became Emperor; Elba, to which he was exiled; and St Helena, where he died.
10. Tristan da Cunha, in the South Atlantic. The nearest land is St Helena, some 1,300 miles to the north-east.

JARGON AND SESQUIPEDALIAN GOBBLEDYGOOK

Some of the following are deliberate examples of circumlocution. The others will be recognised as favourites of those in government, the groves of academe, particularly in the social sciences, and other recondite fields. How many can you put into correct, simple English?

1. Prior to, anterior to.
2. Precipitation entails negation of economy.
3. Viable.
4. The initiation of the termination.
5. Radiation enhancement weapon.
6. Solar bodies tend to exhibit, with respect to and from the viewpoint of their satellites, an apparent orientality of anabasis.
7. Dichotomy.
8. In every canine lifespan is manifested a period of optimum euphoria.
9. Don't initiate protective reaction prior to establishment of firm eyeball identification.
10. 'It is not an avocation of a remunerative description,' in the memorable words of Mr Micawber in *David Copperfield*.

JARGON AND SESQUIPEDALIAN GOBBLEDYGOOK

1. Before.
2. Haste makes waste.
3. Possible, practical, feasible.
4. The beginning of the end.
5. The Pentagon term for the neutron bomb, which kills every living creature within its reach but leaves inanimate structures unharmed.
6. The sun rises in the east.
7. Split, division.
8. Every dog has his day.
9. Don't fire until you see the whites of their eyes.
10. 'In other words, it does *not* pay.' (Mr Micawber was then 'engaged in the sale of corn upon commission'.)

LAST WORDS

Can you identify the people who uttered these dying words?

1. Calling for champagne, he said, 'I am dying, as I have lived, beyond my means.'
2. 'The executioner is, I believe, very expert, and my neck is very slender.'
3. As he considered himself a burden to his companions, he walked out of the tent in a blizzard, saying, 'I am just going outside and may be some time.' He never returned.
4. 'Well, what *is* the answer?' A long pause. Then: 'But what, then, is the question?'
5. To his Flag Captain: 'Kiss me, Hardy. Thank God I have done my duty.' (It has been conjectured that he might have said, 'Kismet, Hardy.')
6. 'Turn up the lights. I don't want to go home in the dark.'
7. In reply to a suggestion that Queen Victoria come to his deathbed: 'Why should I see her? She will only want to give a message to Albert.'
8. 'Only one man ever understood me.' Then, after a pause: 'And he didn't understand me.'
9. 'So little done, so much to do.'
10. 'It has all been very interesting.'

LAST WORDS

1. Oscar Wilde, 1854–1900, the Irish poet, wit, and dramatist.
2. Anne Boleyn, 1507–1536, second wife of Henry VIII.
3. Lawrence E. G. Oates, 1880–1912, a member of the Scott expedition to the South Pole.
4. Gertrude Stein, 1874–1946, American author and patron of the arts.
5. Horatio, Viscount Nelson, 1758–1805, English admiral and hero of the Battle of Trafalgar.
6. William Sidney Porter (O. Henry), 1862–1910, American short-story writer.
7. Benjamin Disraeli, first Earl of Beaconsfield, 1804–1881, British statesman and author.
8. Georg Wilhelm Friedrich Hegel, 1770–1831, German philosopher.
9. Cecil Rhodes, 1853–1902.
10. Lady Mary Wortley Montagu, 1689–1762, English author noted for her highly descriptive letters.

THE LONG AND THE SHORT OF IT

1. How long is an aeon?
2. Where did short-horn cattle originate?
3. Who wrote *Tales of a Wayside Inn*?
4. Just how short is a short wave?
5. Name the pirate leader in Stevenson's *Treasure Island*.
6. Which seventeenth-century English philosopher described the life of man as 'solitary, poor, nasty, brutish and short'?
7. Whose autobiographical masterpiece was *Long Day's Journey into Night*?
8. Who was of the opinion that 'Short words are best and the old words when short are best of all.'?
9. What is the longest word in the unabridged *Oxford English Dictionary*?
10. Can you name seven short men who were engaged in the mining business?

THE LONG AND THE SHORT OF IT

1. An eternity.
2. In northern England, where they are also called Durham cattle.
3. Henry Wadsworth Longfellow.
4. It is an electromagnetic wave with a wavelength of 80 metres or less.
5. Long John Silver.
6. Thomas Hobbes, in *Leviathan*.
7. The American playwright Eugene O'Neill.
8. It was a saying of Winston Churchill's.
9. Floccinaucinihilipilification, which is the action or habit of estimating as useless.
10. Doc, Happy, Grumpy, Dopey, Sleepy, Sneezy, and Bashful, in Walt Disney's classic *Snow White and the Seven Dwarfs*.

MANNERS AND MORES

1. Who wrote a book, subtitled *The Blue Book of Social Usage*, which featured such personages as the Mmes Kindhart, Toplofty, Wellborn, and Cravin Praise; the Oldnames, the Upstarts, the Highbrows, and the Once-weres; 'Bobo' Gilding, and Constance Style; Mr Stocksan Bonds, Jim Smartlington, the genial Clubwin Doe, and that archbounder Richan Vulgar?
2. What are the two magic expressions of etiquette?
3. At a church wedding, why is it customary for the bride to take the right arm of her father?
4. In setting the table for a formal dinner, should one place the napkin to the left or right of the place setting?
5. Should you be presented to the Queen, what is the correct form to be observed?
6. After the ladies have withdrawn from the dinner table, to which direction should the gentlemen pass the port?
7. When a man is walking with a lady in the city, why is it considered polite for him to take the curb side of the pavement?
8. In which countries is it correct to belch following a meal?
9. With which hand do the Arabian desert nomads eat?
10. Speech may, or may not, be a 'mirror of the soul', in the words of Publilius, yet it is by one's speech that one is most readily known. The words and phrases that follow are generally considered to be in bad taste, pretentious, or, in the memorable usage popularised by Nancy Mitford, 'Non-U' ('U' standing for upper-class speech). Give the correct form for the following:
    a) Wealthy
    b) Passed away
    c) Serviette
    d) Note-paper
    e) Horse-riding
    f) Pleased to meet you

MANNERS AND MORES

1. Emily Post, the author of *Etiquette*.
2. 'Please' and 'Thank you'.
3. Because this enables the father to reach the front pew on the left (the bride's side) without crossing the bride's train.
4. Neither. The napkin should be folded flat and laid on each 'place' plate.
5. You should never initiate conversation. When replying, however, you should use in the first instance the title 'Your Majesty', and subsequently 'Ma'am'.
6. To the left.
7. The custom dates from the Middle Ages, when slops were emptied from the windows of the houses on to the street below. The person walking farthest from the street had less chance of being hit.
8. In China and Japan and many of the Pacific nations, where it is a sign of appreciation of the food.
9. Only the right, the left being considered unsanitary because of its associations with eliminative functions. (It will be apparent, in this context, why having one's hand cut off is one of the ultimate degradations in the Arab world.)
10. The following terms are considered 'U' as opposed to 'Non-U':

    a) Rich
    b) Died
    c) Table-napkin
    d) Writing-paper
    e) Riding
    f) How do you do

MEDICINE

1. What is rhinoplasty?
2. When should the Heimlich manoeuvre be used on a person?
3. When would a doctor use a trepan?
4. In what campaign did Dr Paul Ehrlich's 'magic bullet' play an important part?
5. What is a placebo, and what does it literally mean?
6. What is the best cure for circadian disrhythmia?
7. What is the 'king's evil'?
8. Who were the three men who shared the 1945 Nobel Prize for Physiology and Medicine for their work on penicillin?
9. What kind of doctor was Frankenstein?
10. Do you know the origin of the phrase 'Caesarean section', for the delivery of a baby by abdominal incision?

MEDICINE

1. Plastic surgery of the nose.
2. When the person is choking on food. To dislodge the food, you stand behind the victim, then make a fist with one hand and place the fist at the top of the victim's abdomen, just under the rib cage. Grasp your fist with the other hand and give a quick upward thrust. Slapping someone on the back should be avoided as it only aggravates the choking problem.
3. In brain surgery. A trepan is a crown, or cylindrical, saw for perforating the skull.
4. The war against syphilis. Dr Ehrlich discovered salvarsan, which proved effective in the treatment of the disease.
5. A substance with no medication, given simply to humour a patient. In Latin *placebo* means 'I shall please'.
6. Rest probably. The term circadian disrhythmia (Latin *circa*, about, and *dies*, day) means jet lag, or the disruption of bodily rhythms by rapidly changing time zones.
7. Scrofula, a skin disease which the touch of a reigning monarch is supposed to cure.
8. Sir Alexander Fleming, Sir Howard Florey and Sir Ernst Chain.
9. He was not a doctor, nor even a medical student. His fields of study were natural science and mathematics.
10. It is certainly not derived from Julius Caesar, who had a normal birth, though the family name probably derived from such an operation. The phrase probably had its origin in the Latin *a caeso matris utere*, from the incised womb of his mother, from *caesus*, past participle of *caedere*, to cut.

MENU NOTES

1. As a first course Hors d'oeuvre are always appropriate. What does the term literally mean?
2. How did the term 'Newburg' for a type of seafood dish, such as Lobster Newburg, come into being?
3. On a Scottish menu you might find Cock-a-Leekie, Arbroath Smokies, and Atholl Brose. What are these dishes?
4. Whose chef first served Chicken Marengo?
5. Can you translate *Hasenpfeffer mit Kartoffelpuffer*, which might appear on the menu of a Munich restaurant?
6. The famous chef Escoffier while working at the *Hôtel de Paris* in Monaco, created a special dessert for a noted Australian soprano. What was it, and who was she?
7. Why might *Omelette Norvégienne* be a nice touch to conclude a dinner at Lasserre in Paris?
8. Or perhaps you would prefer the multi-layered pastry called a napoleon. How did its name arise?
9. To go with any or all of the above, you could do worse than to order two bottles of 'The Widow' '69, which the *sommelier* would interpret as what?
10. On supper menus as a savoury the familiar melted cheese on toast dish appears variously as 'Welsh Rarebit' and 'Welsh Rabbit'. Which is the correct spelling?

MENU NOTES

1. 'Outside the work' – that is, before the main course. In this usage the word *oeuvre* is always spelt in the singular.
2. This dish was originally called Seafood Wenberg after Ben Wenberg, a New York shipping merchant who invented it and supplied the cayenne, a vital ingredient. It first appeared at the renowned Delmonico's in New York. After an argument with Wenberg, Delmonico renamed the dish 'Newberg' by transposing the first three letters of Wenberg. The word now is generally spelt 'Newburg'.
3. Chicken and leek soup, smoked haddock, and a cream and whisky-flavoured pudding.
4. Napoleon's chef, from the ingredients at hand following the Battle of Marengo in north-western Italy in 1800, when Napoleon defeated the Austrians.
5. It is a rich hare stew with potato pancakes.
6. Peach Melba, after Dame Nellie Melba. (Melba Toast was also named in her honour.)
7. It is Baked Alaska (ice cream covered with meringue and browned in the oven).
8. The pastry is of Italian origin and is a corruption of *napolitain*. It has nothing whatsoever to do with the emperor. In France the dessert is known as *mille feuilles*.
9. Veuve Clicquot – a fine dry champagne of the 1969 vintage. (*Veuve* means 'widow' in French.)
10. Welsh Rabbit. It is a humorous phrase, playing on the poverty of the Welsh. Through failure to understand the joke, writers of menus and cookery books commonly call the dish 'Welsh Rarebit'. Contrary to the general view, Welsh Rabbit is not a corruption of Rarebit, but rather the reverse is true. As Fowler says in *Modern English Usage*: 'Welsh Rabbit is amusing and right, and Welsh Rarebit is stupid and wrong.'

MIND OVER MATTER

1. Who was Psyche?
2. What is the origin of the word 'paranoia'?
3. Who is regarded as the father of psycho-analysis?
4. What phenomenon has been explored scientifically on a large scale by J. B. Rhine, of Duke University?
5. From which organ of the body is the word 'hysteria' derived?
6. Name the psychological test which uses the subject's interpretation of a series of abstract designs to analyse personality traits.
7. Can you differentiate between the ego and the id?
8. For which type of psychology is Carl Gustav Jung noted?
9. Will Schutz is a behavioural psychologist whose first book, *Joy*, introduced which contemporary idea?
10. How many of the following fancies and fears can you identify?

    a) Acrophobia
    b) Ailuromania
    c) Ergophobia
    d) Agoraphobia
    e) Monophobia

    f) Dromomania
    g) Stygiophobia
    h) Eleutheromania
    i) Gynephobia
    j) Pantophobia

MIND OVER MATTER

1. In classical mythology, she was the maiden who was loved by Eros. The name personified the soul. In medical terminology, the prefix 'psych-' means the mind.
2. The Greek words *para* (meaning beyond or beside) and *noos* (meaning the mind).
3. Sigmund Freud.
4. Parapsychology, which includes the study of such psychic phenomena as clairvoyance, telepathy, psychokinensis and extra-sensory perception.
5. The uterus, from the Greek word *hystera*. Since women were considered more unstable than men, it was believed that hysteria must be caused by some purely female organ.
6. The Rorschach test.
7. According to Freud, the ego is the conscious mind, which rules one's behaviour, while the id is the unknown and unconscious mind.
8. Analytical psychology, emphasising the importance of racial and cultural inheritance to a person's development.
9. The encounter group, to develop awareness and encourage non-verbal communication.
10.
   a) Fear of heights
   b) Love of cats
   c) Morbid fear of working
   d) Fear of open spaces
   e) Fear of being alone
   f) Compulsive travelling
   g) Fear of Hell
   h) Mad zeal for freedom
   i) Abnormal fear of women
   j) Fear of everything

MONEY

1. According to the Bible, what is 'the root of all evil'?
2. Why are the edges of gold and silver coins milled?
3. From what is the word 'dollar' derived?
4. What was the first coin to be introduced preparatory to Britain going decimal, and in what year did it go into circulation?
5. What was called 'Seward's Folly' and how much did it cost the United States?
6. The term 'Dixie', for the South, is said to have had what monetary origin?
7. With which countries are the following currencies associated: schilling, sol, won, quetzal, dirham, and baht?
8. Who observed that no one ever went broke by under-estimating the taste of the American public?
9. With which American University do you particularly associate Milton Friedman and the so-called monetarist school of economists?
10. What was the observation of the fabulously rich Nubar Gulbenkian, an Englishman of Armenian extraction, on his custom-built London taxicab, which was tall enough for him to sit in without removing his top hat?

MONEY

1. Not money, but 'the love of money'. – Timothy 6:10.
2. So that it will be apparent if any metal has been filed or cut away.
3. It comes from the German *taler*, which is short for *Joachimstaler*, an early Germanic coin, minted from silver mined in St Joachim's Valley.
4. The two-shilling piece, or florin, introduced in 1849. This scheme was dropped, and Britain did not switch to decimal currency until 1971.
5. William Seward was the Secretary of State who negotiated the purchase of Alaska from the Russians in 1867 for $7.2 million. It was also called 'Seward's Icebox' and 'Seward's Polar Bear Garden'.
6. When Louisiana became a state, bilingual ten-dollar bills were printed with *dix* ('ten' in French) on one side. These bills were called dixies, and the term originally applied to New Orleans. The popularity of the song 'Dixie' expanded the term to include all of the South.
7. Austria, Peru, South Korea, Guatemala, Morocco and United Arab Emirates, and Thailand, respectively.
8. H. L. Mencken, American editor, author and critic.
9. University of Chicago.
10. 'They tell me it turns on a sixpence, whatever that is.'

MUSIC

1. A sackbut was an early form of which musical instrument?
2. By what names are Beethoven's third, sixth, and ninth symphonies known?
3. The words of Yale's 'Whiffenpoof Song' were adapted from which poem by a famous English author?
4. Which musician surrendered his wife to his best friend, who was a famous composer?
5. How many keys are there on a standard piano?
6. Who was the composer of the hymn 'Onward, Christian Soldiers'?
7. In which cathedral cities is the annual Three Choirs Festival held?
8. Who has been called history's most justifiably neglected composer, who had enough daring and ignorance to write for both the double reed slide music stand and the left-handed sewer flute simultaneously, using their incompatibility as a structural element in the composition?
9. To the tune of what song was 'The Battle Hymn of the Republic' set?
10. Whose band do you associate with each of the following signature tunes or themes?

   a) 'One O'Clock Jump'
   b) 'Somebody Stole My Gal'
   c) 'I'm Getting Sentimental Over You'
   d) 'Take the "A" Train'
   e) 'It's Just the Time for Dancing'/'Here's to the Next Time'
   f) 'Listen to My Music'
   g) 'In the Mood'
   h) 'Moonlight Serenade'
   i) 'You're Dancing on My Heart'
   j) 'Rhapsody in Blue'

MUSIC

1. The trombone.
2. The *Eroica*, the *Pastoral*, and the *Choral*, respectively.
3. 'Gentlemen-Rankers', from Rudyard Kipling's *Barrack Room Ballads*.
4. Hans von Bülow, to Richard Wagner, who fathered three children by Cosima von Bülow before they married.
5. Eighty-eight – 52 white, 36 black.
6. Sir Arthur Sullivan, of Gilbert and Sullivan fame.
7. Gloucester, Hereford, and Worcester, in rotation.
8. P. D. Q. Bach, the last and unquestionably the least of the great Johann Sebastian Bach's many children, whose definitive biography has been written by Prof. Schickele. Among his many works deserving of obscurity is Pervertimento in C major for strings, bagpipes, bicycles and balloons.
9. That of 'John Brown's Body'.
10.
    a) Count Basie
    b) Billy Cotton
    c) Tommy Dorsey
    d) Duke Ellington
    e) Henry Hall
    f) Ted Heath
    g) Joe Loss
    h) Glenn Miller
    i) Victor Sylvester
    j) Paul Whiteman

NAVAL AND NAUTICAL LORE

1. Do you know the Latin origin for the word 'captain'?
2. Who had 'the face that launched a thousand ships, And burnt the topless towers of Ilium,' in the words of Marlowe?
3. What was the advice on success given by Sir Joseph Porter, First Lord of the Admiralty, in Gilbert and Sullivan's HMS *Pinafore*?
4. What was the name of Lord Howard of Effingham's flagship when he commanded the fleet that fought the Spanish Armada?
5. A watch at sea is normally for a four-hour period, with the half-hour periods being noted by the ship's bell ringing from one to eight. How did this practice come about?
6. What special flag is flown by an admiral in the Royal Navy?
7. What was the port side of a ship originally called, and why was the name changed?
8. During the American Civil War the first battle in history between two ironclad vessels took place. What were their names?
9. What is a scuttlebutt, and why does the word mean rumour or gossip?
10. The Royal Navy's first 'all big gun' battleship and first nuclear-powered submarine had the same name. What was it?

NAVAL AND NAUTICAL LORE

1. The Latin word *caput*, meaning 'head'.
2. According to Greek mythology, it was Helen, wife of Menelaus of Sparta. Her abduction by Paris brought on the Trojan War.
3.   'Now landsmen all, whoever you may be,
   If you want to rise to the top of the tree,
   If your soul isn't fettered to an office stool,
   Be careful to be guided by this golden rule –
   Stick close to your desks and never go to sea,
   And you all may be Rulers of the Queen's Navee!'
4. *Ark Royal*, the first ship to bear that name.
5. Because the passage of time was originally noted by a half-hour glass.
6. The St George's flag.
7. Larboard. It was changed because of its similarity in sound to starboard. (The 'star' in starboard derives from the Anglo-Saxon *steor*, meaning the 'rudder', which was originally located over the right-hand side of the stern.)
8. Not the *Monitor* and the *Merrimack*, but the *Monitor* (North) and the *Virginia* (South). The latter was originally called the *Merrimack* when it was abandoned by the North, but was renamed when taken by the South and rebuilt. The battle between the two ships ended in a draw. Their ironclad design, with screw propulsion and the *Merrimack*'s turret-mounted guns, was to revolutionise naval warfare over the next century.
9. A cask with a bunghole cut in it, kept on deck to hold water for drinking. It was here that sailors would gather to exchange the latest rumour.
10. HMS *Dreadnought*.

OSCARS

The Academy of Motion Picture Arts and Sciences, which was founded in 1927 with Douglas Fairbanks as its first president, began the distribution of their coveted Academy Awards in 1929. These golden statuettes have been called 'Oscars' since 1931.

1. The first Academy Award for Best Picture went to which film?
2. Who won more Oscars than any other person?
3. The only Academy Award made of wood was given to whom?
4. Only one actor has won Oscars for Best Actor and Best Supporting Actor. Can you name him and the pictures involved?
5. Who is the only performer to be nominated 11 times for an Academy Award and to win three Oscars for starring roles?
6. What do the following have in common: Walter Huston, Kirk Douglas, Judy Garland, Ryan O'Neal, and Henry Fonda?
7. Who has refused to accept an Oscar?
8. Which performer managed to win Academy Awards for playing three parts in two films?
9. Is it possible for an X certificate film to win an award for Best Picture?
10. Which widely acclaimed actor, who was nominated 10 times, won an Oscar for Best Actor, a Special Award, and an Honorary Award?

OSCARS

1. *Wings*, a film about the early days of aviation. It was directed by William Wellman, and featured Richard Arlen, Clara Bow, Charles 'Buddy' Rogers, and Gary Cooper.
2. Walt Disney, with a total of 31 Oscars, excluding scientific or technical awards.
3. Edgar Bergen (and Charlie McCarthy).
4. Jack Lemmon, for his roles as a confused businessman in *Save the Tiger* and as an inept ensign in *Mister Roberts*.
5. Katharine Hepburn. She won Oscars for *Morning Glory, Guess Who's Coming to Dinner*, and *The Lion in Winter*.
6. They are all parents of Oscar winners: John Huston, for direction and screenplay of *The Treasure of the Sierra Madre*; Michael Douglas, as producer of *One Flew Over the Cuckoo's Nest*; and Liza Minelli, Tatum O'Neal, and Jane Fonda as performers.
7. George C. Scott, for *Patton*, and Marlon Brando for *The Godfather*. (Sasheen Littlefeather refused it for Brando.)
8. Fredric March, for his roles in *Dr Jekyll and Mr Hyde* and *The Best Years of Our Lives*.
9. Yes. *Midnight Cowboy*, which won in 1969, was an X certificate film.
10. Laurence Olivier, who in 1948 received an Oscar for Best Actor in *Hamlet*. In 1946 he was given a Special Award for outstanding achievement as actor, producer, and director in bringing *Henry V* to the screen, and in 1979 an Honorary Award 'for the full body of his work, for the unique achievement of his entire career, and his lifetime of contributions to the art of film'.

PAINTING

1. 'Arrangement in Grey and Black No. I' is the title of what famous painting?
2. Which painter set many of his paintings in and around his native village of Cookham in Berkshire?
3. What is the purpose of a maulstick?
4. Whose painting of a sunrise was responsible for the term 'impressionism', which was used derisively at the time?
5. Who wrote a novel based on the life of the French painter Paul Gauguin?
6. What organ did Vincent van Gogh cut off at Christmas time and give to Rachel, a girl in a *maison de tolérance* (a licensed brothel)?
7. Do you know the more familiar names of Sanzio, Vecellio, and Buonarroti?
8. Where do Lawrence's 'Pinky' and Gainsborough's 'Blue Boy' face each other?
9. Which American painter became President of the Royal Academy in London?
10. Who wrote this passage?

   'I must say I like bright colours . . . I rejoice with the brilliant ones, and am genuinely sorry for the poor browns. When I get to heaven. I want to spend a considerable portion of my first million years in painting, and so get to the bottom of the subject. But then I shall require a still gayer palette than I get here below. I expect orange and vermilion will be the darkest, dullest colours upon it, and beyond them there will be a whole range of wonderful new colours which will delight the celestial eye.'

PAINTING

1. Whistler's portrait of his mother. ('Arrangement in Grey and Black No. II' is a portrait of Thomas Carlyle.)
2. Sir Stanley Spencer. A gallery of his work was opened in Cookham in 1962.
3. It is a long wooden stick used by painters to support the hand that holds the brush. One end of the stick is usually covered with something soft like leather to protect the canvas.
4. Claude Monet whose painting was entitled 'Impression, sunrise. A view of the harbour at Le Havre'.
5. W. Somerset Maugham, *The Moon and Sixpence*.
6. His right ear.
7. Raphael, Titian, and Michelangelo, respectively.
8. At the Huntington Library and Art Gallery in San Marino, California.
9. Benjamin West.
10. Winston S. Churchill in *Painting as a Pastime*.

PAIRS

1. Which famous pair of lovers were brought together by a lascivious intermediary named Pandarus, from whom the word 'pander' is derived?
2. According to legend, who were suckled by a she-wolf and later founded what great city?
3. What would you need to visit the Biblical ruins of Sodom and Gomorrah?
4. What is the legend of Pygmalion and Galatea, and which famous musical was based on it?
5. Who were Chang and Eng?
6. Who strolled along the beach and later dined famously on bread and oysters, with pepper and vinegar?
7. Can you name the title characters from *The Two Gentlemen of Verona* in Shakespeare's play?
8. Why is it terrible to be caught between Scylla and Charybdis?
9. What did the intensively-studied families of the Jukes and the Kallikaks have in common?
10. For which profession did Burke and Hare provide a particular service?

PAIRS

1. Troilus and Cressida, whose romance has been told by Boccaccio, Chaucer, and Shakespeare.
2. The twins, Romulus and Remus. Rome.
3. Diving equipment, since, if they exist, they lie buried under lava and the Dead Sea.
4. Pygmalion, a king of Cyprus, hated women but sculpted a statue of such beauty that he fell in love with it. Aphrodite brought the statue to life as Galatea.
   My Fair Lady, by Lerner and Loewe, was based on the play *Pygmalion*, by George Bernard Shaw.
5. The most famous of conjoined twins, they were born in Siam of Chinese parents in 1811 and were known as the Siamese Twins when they were exhibited in P. T. Barnum's circus. Later they married and fathered 22 children.
6. The Walrus and the Carpenter, from *Through the Looking-Glass*, by Lewis Carroll.
7. Valentine and Proteus.
8. Because by avoiding one, you invite destruction by the other. In Greek mythology they were personified as female monsters who were often a peril to mariners. In reality Scylla is a huge rock off the toe of Italy, and across the Strait of Messina is Charybdis, a whirlpool off the Sicilian coast.
9. Feeble-mindedness, with a high incidence of crime and disease. The names were pseudonyms for two US families which were studied to determine the influence of heredity.
10. The medical profession. They were celebrated grave robbers who provided the medical schools of Edinburgh with fresh cadavers for anatomical study. They not only robbed graves but also smothered living victims to ensure fresh delivery.

PHILOSOPHY

1. Its Greek roots give what meaning to the word 'philosophy'?
2. Which famous Greek philosopher always wrote in the form of a dialogue, and who was his teacher?
3. What was the 'Philosopher's Stone'?
4. Which philosopher and mathematician coined the phrase, 'Cogito ergo sum' (I think, therefore I am)?
5. Name the authors of *System of Logic* and *Critique of Pure Reason*.
6. The words 'epicure' and 'epicurean' have a connotation of 'eat, drink, and be merry'. Is this in keeping with the teaching of the Greek philosopher, Epicurus, from whom the words are derived?
7. Which doctrine maintains that the value of any external fact or possession or experience depends on the way in which we take it?
8. Give the title of Sir Thomas More's most famous work, one which contributed a new word to the English language.
9. What was the philosophic and literary movement that flourished in New England in the nineteenth century and led its thinkers to the mystical belief in individualism and the harmony of all things in nature?
10. Which French writer was a leading exponent of twentieth-century exlstentialism, whereby man is free and totally responsible for what he makes of himself?

PHILOSOPHY

1. The love of wisdom, from *philos*, love, and *sophia*, wisdom.
2. Plato. Socrates.
3. A mineral sought by alchemists, that would transmute base metals into gold.
4. René Descartes in *Discours de la Méthode*.
5. John Locke and Immanuel Kant, respectively.
6. No. Although Epicurus defined philosophy as the art of making life happy, with pleasure as the highest and only good, he did not consider pleasure as heedless indulgence but the opposite, with serenity manifesting itself in the avoidance of pain. As a man, Epicurus was extremely frugal and was ordinarily satisfied with bread and water.
7. Stoic self-control by law.
8. *Utopia*, from the Greek for 'nowhere'. More envisaged a land of perfection in social, moral and political life.
9. Transcendentalism.
10. Jean-Paul Sartre.

PICK A NUMBER

1. How many wives did Henry VIII have? Can you name them?
2. What is a baker's dozen, and how did the phrase come about?
3. John Buchan wrote a thrilling spy novel, later made into a film, which had what numerical title?
4. Can you give within 98 miles (157 km) the circumference of the earth at the equator?
5. What house is sometimes known as 'NUMBER ONE, LONDON'?
6. In A. E. Housman's famous poem, how old was the Shropshire lad who heard a wise man say the following?
   'Give crowns and pounds and guineas
   But not your heart away . . .'
7. How many years elapsed between the two major Jacobite risings in the first half of the eighteenth century?
8. Why is the Book of Numbers in the Old Testament so named?
9. What countries are or were divided by boundaries following the 17th, the 38th, and the 49th parallels of latitude?
10. How many birds were received in the song 'The Twelve Days of Christmas'?

PICK A NUMBER

1. Six. Katharine of Aragon, Anne Boleyn, Jane Seymour, Anne of Cleves, Catherine Howard, and Catherine Parr.
2. Thirteen. In England during the Middle Ages it became customary to avoid the harsh penalties for short-weighing bread to give the customer thirteen loaves for every dozen ordered.
3. *The Thirty-Nine Steps*.
4. 24,902 miles (39,843 kms).
5. Apsley House, at Hyde Park Corner, which at one time belonged to the Duke of Wellington, and now houses the Wellington Museum.
6. 'When I was one-and-twenty'. The poem ends:
   'And I am two-and-twenty
   And ah, 'tis true, 'tis true.'
7. Thirty years, from 'the 'Fifteen' to 'the 'Forty-Five'.
8. Because among the events it records are two 'numberings', or censuses, of the Israelites.
9. North and South Vietnam, North and South Korea, and the United States and Canada, respectively.
10. A hundred and eighty-four: 1 partridge on 12 of the days, 2 turtledoves on 11 of the days, 3 French hens on 10 of the days, 4 calling birds on 9 of the days, 6 geese on 7 of the days, and 7 swans on 6 of the days.

POLITICAL LEADERS

1. Who was first called 'The Father of His Country'?
2. Name the South African soldier and statesman who became a member of the Imperial War Cabinet in London in 1917.
3. Can you identify Miguel Hidalgo?
4. What concert pianist became premier of his country?
5. What British Prime Minister's efforts to redeem fallen women were the despair of his family and friends?
6. Who is called 'the Liberator' in South America?
7. What is the more familiar name of Lord Beaconsfield?
8. To whom did Napoleon refer as 'shit (*merde*) in a silk stocking'?
9. Who was Dzhugashvili?
10. Who characteristically wrote in the preface to his book: 'Every great movement on this globe owes its rise to the great speakers and not to the great writers.'?

POLITICAL LEADERS

1. Cicero.
2. General (later Field Marshal) Jan Christiaan Smuts.
3. He was a humble parish priest who is regarded as the father of Mexican independence.
4. Ignace Paderewski, one of the greatest concert pianists of all time, was premier of Poland in 1919, and in 1940–41, the latter period in exile.
5. William Gladstone.
6. Simón Bolívar.
7. Disraeli.
8. Talleyrand.
9. Stalin.
10. Adolf Hitler, in *Mein Kampf*.

THE PRINTED WORD

1. Who was the first person to print in English?
2. What newspaper's motto is 'All the news that's fit to print'?
3. What was Winston Churchill's assignment in the Boer War?
4. Can you name the largest building in the world devoted entirely to rare books and manuscripts?
5. Who said, 'No man but a blockhead ever wrote, except for money.'?
6. Who wrote the play (later a film) *The Front Page*?
7. Which weekly magazine has the largest circulation in Britain? Which monthly magazine has the largest circulation in the world?
8. In which British cities are the following newspapers published: *The Scotsman*, the *Western Mail*, the *Western Morning News*, and the *Yorkshire Post*?
9. Name the famous flier who worked for *The Daily Planet*.
10. What do the names of the Russian newspapers *Pravda* and *Izvestia* mean in English?

THE PRINTED WORD

1. William Caxton in the fifteenth century. His translation from the French in 1475, *The Recuyell of the Historyes of Troye*, was the first book printed in English.
2. *The New York Times*. The paper adopted the motto at the end of the last century to distinguish itself from the sensationalist yellow press.
3. He was sent to cover it in 1899 as a correspondent for a London newspaper, the *Morning Post*. His dispatches about his capture and imprisonment by the Boers, and subsequent escape, brought him fame at an early age.
4. The Beinecke Rare Book and Manuscript Library at Yale University.
5. Dr Samuel Johnson. Boswell quotes the remark in his *Life of Johnson*.
6. Ben Hecht and Charles MacArthur.
7. *Radio Times. The Reader's Digest.*
8. Edinburgh, Cardiff, Plymouth, and Leeds, respectively.
9. Clark Kent, otherwise known as Superman.
10. *Pravda* means 'Truth', and *Izvestia* means 'News' or 'Information'.

QUARTETS

1. What are the allegorical figures of the Four Horsemen of the Apocalypse in the Bible supposed to represent?
2. What were the four original provinces of the Dominion of Canada?
3. How did plus fours get their name?
4. What are the titles of the poems which make up T. S. Eliot's *Four Quartets*?
5. What is a four-in-hand?
6. Who are Norbert Brainin, Siegmund Nissel, Peter Schidloff and Martin Lovett?
7. In a speech to Congress in 1941 proposing lend-lease legislation, President Roosevelt enunciated the principle of the Four Freedoms, which was later incorporated in the Atlantic Charter. What are the Four Freedoms?
8. Can you give the derivation of the term 'fourflusher' for a braggart or a bluffer?
9. Who was the first man to run a mile in under four minutes?
10. In the *Rubáiyát of Omar Khayyám*, what do *Rubáiyát* and *Khayyám* mean?

QUARTETS

1. It is believed that the rider on the white horse represents Christ; the rider on the black horse is famine; on the red horse is war; and on the pale horse, death.
2. Ontario, Quebec, New Brunswick, and Nova Scotia.
3. Plus fours were a style of knickerbockers which had four inches added to each leg. They were popular for golf in the 'twenties.
4. 'Burnt Norton', 'East Coker', 'The Dry Salvages', and 'Little Gidding'.
5. A coach drawn by four horses, two by two, driven by one person.
6. They are the members of the Amadeus String Quartet.
7. Freedom of speech and expression, freedom of worship, freedom from want, and freedom from fear.
8. The term arises from a poker player with a four-card flush (also called a bobtail flush) bluffing by pretending to have a full flush.
9. Roger Bannister, who in 1954 ran the mile at Oxford in 3 minutes, 59.4 seconds.
10. Quatrains and tentmaker.

REPTILES AND AMPHIBIANS

1. What is the heaviest and longest of all snakes?
2. Which are the only two poisonous lizards in the world?
3. What reptile group protects its nest, eggs and young for up to three years?
4. Who eulogised a particular toad in a song beginning as follows:
     'The world has held great Heroes
       As history books have showed;
      But never a name to go down to fame
        Compared with that of Toad.'
5. How often does a snake shed its skin?
6. Who was catapulted into fame by his story of the jumping frog 'Dan'l Webster'? Dan'l is defeated when the owner of a rival frog pours quail-shot down his gullet.
7. What is the name of the third eyelid, common to reptiles and birds, which moves horizontally across the eye?
8. When a snake sticks out its tongue, what is it doing?
9. Who admired the fertile turtle in the following lines?
     'The turtle lives 'twixt plated decks
      Which practically conceal its sex.
      I think it clever of the turtle
      In such a fix to be so fertile.'
10. The term 'crocodile tears' resulted from the belief that crocodiles weep after eating their victims, and came to mean false tears or an insincere display of grief. What is rather fishy about all this?

REPTILES AND AMPHIBIANS

1. The anaconda, or python, of South America. One specimen shot on the upper Orinoco River measured over 37 feet (11.4 metres).
2. The Gila monster and the Mexican beaded lizard.
3. The crocodile family.
4. The subject of the song, Mr Toad himself, in *The Wind in the Willows*, by Kenneth Grahame.
5. Young snakes may shed as many as 14 times a year, while older ones may shed from three to four times a year.
6. Mark Twain. The sketch was the title piece of a series of stories that formed his first book, *The Celebrated Jumping Frog of Calaveras County*.
7. The nicitating membrane.
8. Smelling.
9. Ogden Nash, in 'The Turtle', from *Many Long Years Ago*.
10. Crocodiles are unable to shed tears as they have no tear glands. Secretions keep their eyes moist.

ROMANCE AND CHIVALRY

1. What was the Holy Grail?
2. How did the Holy Grail come to Europe?
3. How did the knights of the Round Table know Galahad should seek the Grail?
4. Who wrote *Le Morte Darthur* (usually called *Morte d'Arthur*), published by William Caxton in 1485?
5. Which Poet Laureate reconstructed the tale of Arthur, and in what work?
6. What was the name of the dynasty to which Charlemagne belonged?
7. What famous defeat of the forces of Charlemagne was immortalised in the *Chanson de Roland*? In the poem, the victors were Saracens; in fact, they were the fiercely independent Basques.
8. What is meant by the peers of Charlemagne?
9. Where were the Knights of St John expelled from by the Turks in 1523, and where did they find a new home in 1530?
10. Who was the knight *'sans peur et sans reproche'*?

ROMANCE AND CHIVALRY

1. The dish or cup used by Christ at the Last Supper.
2. It was brought by Joseph of Arimathea, who was said to have received it at the Last Supper, and to have caught Christ's blood in it at the Crucifixion.
3. Because he was able to sit in the Siege Perilous.
4. Sir Thomas Malory.
5. Alfred, Lord Tennyson, in *Idylls of the King*.
6. Carlovingian, or Carolingian.
7. Roncesvalles in the Pyrenees.
8. Twelve knights who were of equal rank and were called paladins or knights of the palace.
9. Rhodes, Malta.
10. The Chevalier Bayard (*c*. 1474–1524).

SAINTS AND SINNERS

1. Petite Miquelon and Grande Miquelon are two of three French islands off the coast of Newfoundland. What is the third?
2. Name the seven deadly sins.
3. Which literary figure is customarily depicted in a drawing with a halo above his head?
4. Who was 'more sinn'd against than sinning'?
5. What are the correct names for two Caribbean islands commonly called St Kitts and Statia?
6. Give the author of this epigram entitled 'On His Books':
   'When I am dead, I hope it may be said:
       "His sins were scarlet, but his books were read."'
7. What happened to St Christopher, the patron saint of travellers, in 1969?
8. What are the four cardinal virtues?
9. Can you name the famous jazz song that became popular for funeral marches in New Orleans?
10. Where would you be likely to sin with Elinor Glyn, a writer of torrid love stories in the 1920s?

SAINTS AND SINNERS

1. St Pierre.
2. Pride, lust, envy, anger, covetousness, gluttony and sloth.
3. Simon Templar, in the *Saint* books, by Leslie Charteris.
4. King Lear.
5. St Christopher (British) and Sint Eustatius (Dutch).
6. Hilaire Belloc.
7. His name was dropped from the liturgical calendar.
8. Prudence, justice, temperance and fortitude.
9. 'When the saints go marching in'.
10. Most probably on a skin according to these lines:
    'Would you like to sin
    With Elinor Glyn
    On a tiger skin?
    Or would you prefer
    To err with her
    On some other fur?'

SCIENCE FICTION

1. Why is science fiction considered to be a separate art form from fantasy?
2. Which two European writers, one French and one English, did the most to popularise science fiction?
3. The alleged burning point of paper provided the title for which novel of the future?
4. Who played the part of the Bride of Frankenstein in the film of the same name?
5. Which sixteenth-century Italian poet made monsters called 'orcs' famous?
6. Which science fiction author has written over 200 books on a variety of subjects?
7. The concept of 'Big Brother is watching you' was devised by whom?
8. The word 'robot', a mechanical man or woman, originated in which play?
9. In four film versions of Robert Louis Stevenson's novel *The Strange Case of Dr Jekyll and Mr Hyde*, which four actors played the lead?
10. What major science-fiction writer played a part in the development of radar and forecast the development of the satellite communication network?

SCIENCE FICTION

1. Because in science fiction the events of the story fall within the province of what is deemed future possibility.
2. Jules Verne and H. G. Wells.
3. *Fahrenheit 451*, by Ray Bradbury.
4. Valerie Hobson. (Elsa Lanchester played the bride of the creature.)
5. Ariosto.
6. Isaac Asimov.
7. George Orwell, in *1984*.
8. *R.U.R.* (Rossum's Universal Robots), by Karel Čapek.
9. John Barrymore, Fredric March, Spencer Tracy, and Jack Palance.
10. Arthur C. Clarke.

SHAKESPEARE

1. Who was the Merchant of Venice?
2. In which two plays are these strange stage directions: 'Enter a messenger with two heads and a hand' and 'Exit pursued by a bear'?
3. Are Shakespeare's sonnets addressed to a man or a woman?
4. Who said, 'She should have died hereafter,' and about whom?
5. What do the following plays have in common: *A Midsummer Night's Dream, The Taming of the Shrew, Hamlet,* and *Love's Labour's Lost*?
6. Where would you find Sir Toby Belch and Sir Andrew Aguecheek?
7. What does Hamlet mean by 'nunnery' when he directs Ophelia to 'Get thee to a nunnery!'?
8. Who delivered the seven-ages-of-man speech, and in which play?
9. Give the alternative title of *Twelfth Night*.
10. In which play are the following words (in the original spelling) of Shakespeare to be found?
    'Good friend for Jesus sake forbeare
    To digg the dust encloased heare!
    Blest be ye man yt spares thes stones,
    And curst be he yt moves my bones.'

SHAKESPEARE

1. Antonio, not Shylock.
2. *Titus Andronicus* and *The Winter's Tale*, respectively.
3. Both: most are addressed to a man, the last few to the famous Dark Lady of the Sonnets.
4. Macbeth, of Lady Macbeth.
5. Each contains a play within a play.
6. *Twelfth Night*.
7. It was Elizabethan slang for a whorehouse.
8. Jaques, in *As You Like It*. The passage begins as follows:
   'All the world's a stage,
   And all the men and women merely players:
   They have their exits and their entrances;
   And one man in his time plays many parts,
   His acts being seven ages.'
9. *What You Will*.
10. In none of them. This verse is carved on Shakespeare's tombstone in the Holy Trinity Church at Stratford-on-Avon.

SOUTH AMERICA

1. Why is Brazil the only South American country to use the Portuguese language?
2. In which country is a capital not the seat of government?
3. Where are Panama hats made?
4. Who gave his name to the cold ocean current flowing north along the coasts of Chile and Peru to Ecuador?
5. For what is Portillo noted?
6. In 1894, for spying, Captain Alfred Dreyfus was deported for life to Devil's Island. Where was this infamous penal colony located?
7. A South American country and its principal river have what metal in common?
8. Which is the highest navigable lake in the world?
9. Name the two South American nations which are members of the Organisation of Petroleum Exporting Countries (OPEC).
10. Where did the Marquesa de Montemayor, Uncle Pio, Pepito, Jaime, and Esteban die? Who investigated their deaths?

SOUTH AMERICA

1. This was arranged by a series of agreements, starting with the Treaty of Tordesillas, whereby Spain and Portugal divided the non-Christian world between them. The treaty followed a papal bull issued in 1493 by Pope Alexander VI.
2. Bolivia. Sucre, named after the first elected president of Bolivia, is the constitutional capital; La Paz is the administrative capital.
3. Ecuador. Panama was a distribution centre for the hats.
4. Baron Alexander von Humboldt, German naturalist and explorer.
5. Located in the Chilean Andes, it is the leading ski resort in South America.
6. Off the coast of French Guiana, now an overseas department of France. (Dreyfus was later exonerated, and the penal colony was phased out in 1946.)
7. The names Argentina and Rio de la Plata both refer to silver.
8. Lake Titicaca, on the border between Peru and Bolivia.
9. Venezuela and Ecuador.
10. In the Peruvian Andes when the Bridge of San Luis Rey collapsed. In Thornton Wilder's novel, which won the Pulitzer Prize in 1927, Brother Juniper, a Franciscan, investigated why they were chosen to die.

SPACE

1. In which constellation are the seven stars that form the Plough?
2. What is the most abundant element in the universe?
3. Does the earth rotate on its axis from east to west or from west to east?
4. 'Black holes', the first of which was discovered in 1975, are believed to be what?
5. Who wrote the words and music for 'Stardust'?
6. Which element was discovered in the spectrum of the sun before it was known to exist on earth?
7. What does the abbreviation NASA stand for?
8. Explain the heavenly connection of these characters from Shakespeare's *A Midsummer Night's Dream* and *The Tempest*; Miranda, Ariel, Titania and Oberon.
9. Who was the first man to set foot on the moon in 1969, and what were his memorable words on the occasion?
10. How did the space shuttle *Enterprise* come by its name?

SPACE

1. *Ursa Major*, the 'Great Bear', a constellation in the region of the north celestial pole, near Draco and Leo.
2. Hydrogen.
3. From west to east.
4. Superdense collapsed stars with a gravitational pull so great that even light can escape, making them invisible. They are found by searching for evidence of extreme gravity. Scientists hope that they will tell us more about the life cycle of stars and stellar evolution.
5. Lyrics by Mitchell Parish, music by Hoagy Carmichael.
6. Helium, which is not flammable and second only to hydrogen in lightness. Its name derives from the Greek *helios*, sun.
7. The National Aeronautics and Space Administration, which is located in Houston, Texas.
8. They are all satellites of the planet Uranus.
9. Astronaut Neil Armstrong. 'That's one small step for a man, one giant leap for mankind.' (When this remark was first printed in the newspapers, the indefinite article 'a' was missing, probably having been lost because of static in transmission from the moon. This had the effect of ruining the sense of the line, but Armstrong caught the omission, and the correct version was finally printed.)
10. It took its name from the star ship used in the TV series 'Star Trek'.

A SPELLING TEST FOR THE LITERATE

Mark the words which are misspelt.

accidentally
accommodate
acquiesce
anoint
aquarium
assassin
battalion
beige
boundary
broccoli
calamine
cemetery
consensus
controversy
desiccate
dittos
dyeing (colouring)

ecstasy
embarrass
frolicking
gauge
harass
hypocrisy
innovate
inoculate
kimono
liaison
liquefy
mischievous
moccasin
naphtha
panegyric
parallel
paraffin

plausible
precipitate
pyorrhea
queue
rarefy
reminiscence
sacrilegious
seize
separate
shriek
siege
sizable
supersede
ukelele
vermilion
weird
wield

A SPELLING TEST FOR THE LITERATE

They are all spelt correctly.

SPORTING LIFE

1. What annual European sporting event is seen 'live' by the most spectators?
2. In rodeo competition, what is the standard time required for a rider to stay on in bareback, saddle bronc, and bull-riding events?
3. What does the 2000 signify in the name of the French ski-resort Isola 2000?
4. Canada and Scotland regularly play for the Strathcona Cup in what sport?
5. What popular sport was invented by James Naismith, a YMCA college instructor?
6. In which sport are 'sculls' and 'sweeps' used, and what is the difference?
7. What is the more familiar name of Edson Arantes do Nascimento?
8. What is the distance of the marathon race and why?
9. 'Walking the dog', 'tick-tack', and 'tie hop' are terms used in which activity?
10. In *A Woman of No Importance*, how does Oscar Wilde describe the English country gentleman galloping after a fox?

SPORTING LIFE

1. The Tour de France bicycle race. It is estimated that over its 23 days the race is watched by around fifteen million people.
2. Eight seconds.
3. It denotes that the resort is approximately 2000 metres above sea level.
4. Curling – a game like bowls, played on ice, in which two teams slide heavy oblate stones towards a target circle at either end.
5. Basketball. He invented it to fill the seasonal gap between football in the autumn and baseball in the spring.
6. Rowing. In a scull each rower has two oars, each about 9 feet (3 metres) long. Sculls can be 'singles', 'doubles', 'quads' or 'octopedes'. In a sweep each rower has a 12-foot (4-metre) oar. Sweeps come in 'pairs', 'fours' and 'eights'.
7. Pelé, the famous Brazilian soccer player.
8. In 490 BC the Athenian army, outnumbered ten to one, defeated 100,000 Persians at the Battle of Marathon. A runner brought the news to Athens, which lay some 25 miles (40 kms) away. When the Olympic Games were revived in 1896, a race covering approximately the same distance was included in the events. In 1908, when the Olympics were held in London, the race started at Windsor Castle and ended at the White City Stadium, a distance of 26 miles. King Edward VII insisted that the race finish in front of the Royal Box, which increased the length to 26 miles, 385 yards. This is now the standard distance.
9. Skateboarding.
10. 'The unspeakable in full pursuit of the uneatable.'

STRANGE PRACTICES

1. Can you describe the strange practice known as suttee?
2. The body of which deceased world leader is on daily exhibition?
3. What is a trigamist?
4. Vlad IV, a fifteenth-century prince of Wallachia, was called Vlad the Impaler because of his penchant for impaling his prisoners on wooden stakes when they were still alive. By which name, more familiar in another context, was he also known?
5. In Robert Service's poem, what was the strange thing done 'that night on the marge of Lake Lebarge'?
6. What has occurred in the worship of Juggernaut, whose statue is mounted on an enormous temple cart and dragged by pilgrims in an annual rite?
7. According to the French, what is *le vice anglais*?
8. Define purdah.
9. What is meant by defenestration?
10. Egyptian mummies derived their name from the Arabic word *mumiyah*, meaning what?

STRANGE PRACTICES

1. The act, now forbidden by law, of a Hindu widow cremating herself on her husband's funeral pyre.
2. Lenin, whose embalmed remains may be seen in a transparent casket in a mausoleum outside the Kremlin walls in Moscow.
3. A man with three wives, or a woman with three husbands.
4. Dracula. He was the son of Vlad Dracul (Vlad the Devil) and was called Dracula, or Son of the Devil. Bram Stoker took this name for the title of his famous novel about vampires.
5. 'The Cremation of Sam McGee'.
6. Worshippers are said to have thrown themselves under the immense wheels of the wagon to be crushed to death.
7. Flagellation.
8. It is the Hindu practice of secluding women from men or strangers.
9. An act of throwing someone or something out of a window (Latin *fenestra*, window).
10. Bitumen, because it was once believed that bitumen was used in the process of mummification.

THE THEATRE

1. Name the four most important Greek dramatists. Which one is the exception to the others?
2. With what two celebrated actresses did Bernard Shaw carry on famous correspondences?
3. Which famous portrayer of Hamlet slept in a coffin?
4. What are the names of the three theatres in the National Theatre complex on the South Bank in London?
5. 'Experience is the name everyone gives to their mistakes' is a typical line from a nineteenth-century drawing-room comedy by what author?
6. How did Vladimir and Estragon pass their time, only to be disappointed in the end?
7. Can you name the famous actress whose youthful beauty attracted so many royal protectors that she was called 'the sport of kings'?
8. What is the name of the Broadway Theatre award, and after whom is it named?
9. In December 1660 Margaret Hughes made what is believed to be the first appearance of an actress on the English public stage. What part was she playing?
10. Which musicals featured the following songs? Who were the composers and lyricists?
    a) 'I Hate Men'
    b) 'Cock-Eyed Optimist'
    c) 'Get Me to the Church on Time'
    d) 'It Ain't Necessarily So'
    e) 'Diamonds Are a Girl's Best Friend'

THE THEATRE

1. Aeschylus, Aristophanes, Europides, Sophocles. Aristophanes wrote comedies, the others tragedies.
2. Ellen Terry and Mrs Patrick Campbell.
3. Sarah Bernhardt, whom Oscar Wilde called 'The divine Sarah', a designation by which she became universally known.
4. The Olivier, the Lyttleton, and the Cottesloe.
5. Oscar Wilde, in *Lady Windermere's Fan*.
6. Waiting for Godot, who never appeared, in Samuel Beckett's play.
7. Lillie Langtry, who was known as the Jersey Lily after the island where she was born.
8. The Tony, in honour of Antoinette Perry, the founder of the American Theater Wing.
9. Desdemona, in Shakespeare's *Othello*.
10. a) *Kiss Me Kate*, by Cole Porter
    b) *South Pacific*, by Richard Rodgers and Oscar Hammerstein
    c) *My Fair Lady*, by Alan Jay Lerner and Frederick Loewe
    d) *Porgy and Bess*, by George and Ira Gershwin
    e) *Gentlemen Prefer Blondes*, by Leo Robin and Jule Styne

TRANSPORT

1. What is the function of the mules used at the Panama Canal?
2. A car bearing the initials CH comes from what country?
3. A Nantucket sleigh-ride refers to what?
4. Who made the first successful nonstop flight across the Atlantic Ocean? When?
5. What significant event occurred at Promontory Point, Utah, in 1869?
6. What might the Chunnel be?
7. Of what words is taxicab the shortened form?
8. To whom is the command 'Mush!' given?
9. Why was the first Duke of Wellington opposed to the newly emerging railways in Britain?
10. On what track of the Pennsylvania Station would you find the Chattanooga Choo-Choo?

TRANSPORT

1. Mules are the small electric locomotives used to pull ships through the locks.
2. Switzerland. CH is the abbreviation for the country's formal Latin name, *Confederatio Helvetica*, the Swiss Confederation.
3. A ride in a whaleboat behind a harpooned whale.
4. John Alcock and Arthur Whitten Brown, in 1919, from Newfoundland to Ireland. Both men were subsequently knighted.
5. The completion of the first US transcontinental railway, when the Union Pacific Railroad coming from Nebraska met the Central Pacific from California. They drove a golden spike to celebrate the occasion.
6. A proposed tunnel under the English Channel.
7. *Taximètre-cabriolet.* Taxi is from the French *taxe*, charge, and cabriolet is derived from the Latin *caper*, meaning he-goat, in allusion to the taxi's bounding motion.
8. To a team of sledge-dogs, to make them start or go faster.
9. Because they would encourage the lower orders to move about.
10. Track 29.

WAR

1. Who said, 'There never was a good war or a bad peace.'?
2. The loss of what French city by the English in 1453 ended the Hundred Years' War?
3. Which battle is said to have been won on the playing fields of Eton?
4. To what was Maréchal Bosquet referring when he observed: *'C'est magnifique, mais ce n'est pas la guerre.'* (It's magnificent, but it isn't war.)?
5. What is shrapnel, and how did it get its name?
6. What was a sutler's function in the armies of the past?
7. How did the term 'fifth column', for secret subversives working within a country, come about?
8. Who were referred to as 'the Ladies from Hell'?
9. At what age does a Field Marshal in the British Army retire?
10. From what country do Gurkha soldiers come?

WAR

1. Benjamin Franklin, in a letter to Josiah Quincy, 11 September 1773.
2. Bordeaux. Only Calais remained in English hands.
3. Waterloo. There is no firm evidence, however, that Wellington ever said this.
4. The gallant but foolhardy Charge of the Light Brigade during the Battle of Balaclava in the Crimean War, October 1854. (When oleomargarine was introduced as a substitute for butter in England in 1914, *Punch* magazine commented: *'C'est magnifique, mais ce n'est pas le beurre.'*)
5. An anti-personnel projectile containing metal balls, fused to explode in the air above enemy troops, or the metal balls in such a projectile. It was invented by Lieutenant (later General) Henry Shrapnel, a British artillery officer. Shrapnel should not be confused with shell fragments.
6. A camp follower who peddled provisions to the soldiers.
7. During the Spanish Civil War General Emilio Mola, when he was attacking Madrid, said he was in charge of five columns: four advancing from the outside and 'the fifth column within the city'. Ernest Hemingway popularised the phrase by using it as the title of a play.
8. The kilted Highland regiments of World War I, who went into battle to the death-defying skirl of the pipes.
9. A Field Marshal never retires, but remains on the active list until he dies, though he receives less pay after he ceases to be employed.
10. The Kingdom of Nepal, in the Himalayas.

WATER

1. Name the principal oceans of the world.
2. Which famous French revolutionary was murdered in his bath by whom?
3. Which is the largest lake in the world?
4. Name the author of *The Cruel Sea*.
5. Who wrote the following, and what was the name of the poem?

    I must down to the seas again, to the lonely sea and the sky.

6. Who was surprised in her bath by a pair of lascivious elders who made indecent proposals to her and later fled to cover up their guilt?
7. Locate and describe the Sargasso Sea.
8. What and where is Neptune's Staircase?
9. Who, when bathing, cried 'Eureka!' because he had discovered an important principle of physics? What was the principle involved, and what does 'Eureka' mean?
10. Who says the following?

    'I chatter, chatter as I flow
      To join the brimming river,
    For men may come and men may go,
      But I go on for ever.'

WATER

1. The Atlantic, Pacific, Indian, their southern extensions in Antarctica, and the Arctic.
2. Jean Paul Marat, by Charlotte Corday in 1793. While hiding in the sewers of Paris, Marat contracted a skin disease which required treatments in a warm bath.
3. The Caspian Sea is the largest inland sea or lake in the world, with an area of about 144,000 square miles (230,400 square kms). The fresh-water lake with the greatest surface area, about 31,800 square miles (50,880 square kms), is Lake Superior, one of the Great Lakes.
4. Nicholas Monserrat.
5. John Masefield, 'Sea-Fever'.
6. Susannah, as related in the book of Daniel, from the Apocrypha. The falsity of the elders was subsequently exposed by sharp cross-questioning by Daniel, and they were duly punished. (Apocrypha, Daniel 13)
7. It is a section of the North Atlantic Ocean between the West Indies and the Azores. It is a relatively still area, with an abundance of seaweed in the centre of a great swirl of ocean currents.
8. A series of eight locks at the south-west end of the Caledonian Canal, near Fort William in Scotland.
9. Archimedes, a Greek mathematician, physicist, and inventor, observing the overflow of water in his bath, discovered the principle, known today by his name, that the volume of an irregular solid can be measured by the displacement of water. 'Eureka' (Greek *heureka*) means 'I have found (it).'
10. The Brook, in the poem of the same name by Alfred Lord Tennyson.

WHO SAID IT FIRST?

1. 'If a house be divided against itself, that house cannot stand.'
2. '*L'etat c'est moi.*' (I am the state.)
3. 'Survival of the fittest.'
4. '*Qu'ils mangent de la brioche.*' (Let them eat cake.)
5. 'Make a better mousetrap and the world will beat a path to your door.'
6. '*Ils ne passeront pas.*' (They shall not pass.)
7. 'Murder will out.'
8. 'Iron Curtain.'
9. 'It is now the moment to recall what our country has done for each of us, and to ask ourselves what we can do for our country in return.'
10. 'Any man who hates dogs and babies can't be all bad.'

WHO SAID IT FIRST?

1. Jesus: Mark 3:25. Lincoln used this quotation, slightly changed, in an 1858 speech.
2. Although commonly attributed to Louis XIV, there is no firm evidence to prove that he said it. Napoleon, however, did – in a speech to the French senate in 1814.
3. Herbert Spencer, although Charles Darwin later adopted it.
4. Certainly not Marie Antoinette. It appears in Rousseau's *Confessions* written before she even arrived in France.
5. Emerson wrote in his *Journal*: 'better chairs or knives, crucibles, or church organs,' but never alluded to mousetraps. Nevertheless, the quotation is normally attributed to him.
6. Though often attributed to Marshal Pétain, it seems probable that the phrase was first used by General Nivelle. Its first appearance in print was in an Order of the Day issued during the Battle of Verdun in 1916.
7. Geoffrey Chaucer in *The Canterbury Tales*. In *Hamlet* (Act II, Scene i), Shakespeare wrote: 'For murder though it have no tongue will speak . . .'
8. H. G. Wells, in his science-fiction novel *The Food of the Gods*, published in 1904. The phrase was again employed by Goebbels, Hitler's Minister of Propaganda, during World War II. Churchill popularised the term in his speech at Westminster College, Fulton, Missouri, in 1946, when he said, 'From Stettin in the Baltic to Trieste in the Adriatic an iron curtain has descended across the Continent.'
9. Oliver Wendell Holmes, Jr., in an address given in 1884. Warren G. Harding also expressed the same thought, which, however, is best remembered from John F. Kennedy's inaugural address: '. . . Ask not what your country can do for you; ask what you can do for your country.'
10. It was not said by W. C. Fields, but about him, by Leo Rosten, at a banquet for Fields in 1939.

THE WILD WEST

1. Who authorised negotiations for the Louisiana Purchase in 1803?
2. In which state is the Donner Pass, and for what is it known?
3. Who was engaged in the shoot-out in 1881 at the O.K. Corral in Tombstone, Arizona?
4. Can you describe a Buntline Special?
5. Why are John Sutter and his mill famous?
6. The fringe on buckskin shirts and jackets served what effective purpose?
7. How many acres of unoccupied public land were granted to a settler under the Homestead Act of 1862?
8. Can you give the origin of the word 'cowpoke'?
9. In the fur trade, what were 'hairy bank notes'?
10. What was the name of the notorious character who is reputed to have had 12 husbands, who dressed, cursed and shot like a man, and who was buried beside Wild Bill Hickok in Deadwood, South Dakota?

THE WILD WEST

1. President Thomas Jefferson.
2. California, high up in the Sierra Nevada. It was there that a group of 87 emigrants, including two Donner families, were trapped in the snow during the winter of 1846–47. Only half survived, and the remaining members were driven to cannibalism.
3. The Earps (Wyatt and his brothers, Morgan and Virgil) and Doc Holliday versus the Clanton and McLaury brothers.
4. It is a long-barrelled, 12-inch variant of the two most popular pistols of the West: the .44 and .45 Colt single-action revolvers. Novelist Ned Buntline gave these to Wyatt Earp, Bat Masterson, and others.
5. It was the discovery of gold at Sutter's Mill that started the California gold rush.
6. It helped to shed the rainwater.
7. The Act provided for the transfer of a quarter-square-mile section of 160 acres to each homesteader on payment of a nominal fee after five years of residence.
8. One of his duties was to poke the cattle in the trailers to keep them on their feet so that the trailer could be filled to capacity on its way to the market. Of course, he also poked or punched cattle to keep them moving on the range.
9. Beaver pelts: just as a buck, short for the buckskin used in trade, has come to mean a dollar.
10. Martha Jane Canary, otherwise known as Calamity Jane, who boasted of her exploits as stagecoach driver, pony express rider, and scout with Custer's forces.

WINE

1. Is Chablis a red or white wine? A Bordeaux or a Burgundy?
2. What do the initials VSOP stand for that are found on some brandies?
3. The names of most Alsatian wines contain what sort of information?
4. The indentation on the bottom of some wine bottles, which is called a kick or a punt, serves what two purposes?
5. What was the name of the insect that devastated European vineyards in the second half of the last century?
6. Name the two South American countries which produce good to excellent wines that are relatively inexpensive?
7. Which city in Spain lends its name to the fortified wine known as sherry?
8. The finest Chianti 'Classico', which may carry the symbol of the Black Rooster on the label, is produced where in Italy?
9. Who drew the famous *New Yorker* cartoon of a host at a dinner party proudly explaining to his guests, 'It's a naïve domestic Burgundy without any breeding, but I think you'll be amused by its presumption.'?
10. Champagne comes in a wide selection of sizes. Can you name eight of the ten bottle sizes and the amount of wine in each?

WINE

1. Chablis is a white Burgundy. It is also a generic name for bulk wine in many other, non-European parts of the world, including the United States and Canada.
2. Very Special (or Superior) Old Pale.
3. The grape variety from which they are made, such as Riesling or Sylvaner, rather than a vineyard or village.
4. To strengthen the bottle and to catch sediment in the wine.
5. Phylloxera vitifoliae, grape phylloxera.
6. Argentina and Chile.
7. Jerez de la Frontera. The wine was formerly pronounced 'sherris' from Xeres, the older name of Jerez, dating from the Moorish conquest.
8. In a specific geographical district located between Florence and Siena.
9. James Thurber.
10. Usually available are:

1)	Nip or split	¼ bottle
2)	Half bottle	½ bottle
3)	Quart	1 bottle
4)	Magnum	2 bottles
5)	Jeroboam	4 bottles

   After the jeroboam come the curiosities. Because of their size, it is not practical to produce champagne in them, and they are generally filled from a number of smaller bottles.

6)	Rehoboam	6 bottles
7)	Methuselah	8 bottles
8)	Salmanazar	12 bottles
9)	Balthazar	16 bottles
10)	Nebuchadnezzar	20 bottles

WORD ORIGINS

Can you give the derivation of the following words?
1. Alphabet
2. Chortle
3. Quintessence
4. Tantalise
5. Bedlam
6. Sophomore
7. Piggyback
8. Pandemonium
9. Supercilious
10. Tawdry

WORD ORIGINS

1. It is simply a word combining the first two letters of the Greek alphabet – *alpha* and *beta*.
2. Meaning 'to chuckle throatily'. The word, a blend of 'chuckle' and 'snort', was coined by Lewis Carroll in the poem about the Jabberwock in *Through the Looking-Glass.*
3. The fifth essence which formed the basis of the stars. The Greeks added this to the four elements: earth, air, fire and water.
4. Tantalise is derived from Tantalus, a king of Greek mythology, whom Zeus punished by immersing him in water with fine fruit above his head. When he tried to drink or eat, either the water receded or the fruit rose above his reach.
5. This is simply a contraction of St Mary of Bethlehem, the name of an insane asylum in medieval London, and refers to the din made by the inmates.
6. One who is literally half wise and half foolish, from the Greek *sophos*, wise, and *moros*, foolish.
7. Originally pick-a-pack, similar to putting a knapsack on one's shoulders. When children were so carried, they changed the word to their own liking.
8. This is a word coined by John Milton in *Paradise Lost* for the capital of Hell. He formed it from the Greek *pan*, all, and *daimon*, demon. It passed into general use from the idea that Hell is a place of uproar and wild confusion.
9. Supercilious is a word characterised by scorn or disdain and is often accompanied by a raising of the eyebrows, which is how the word came about: from the Latin *super*, above, and *cilium*, eyelid.
10. Tawdry lace, originally St Audrey's lace, was a silk 'lace' or neck-tie worn by women in the sixteenth and early seventeenth centuries. Cheap and showy qualities of the lace were produced for sale at St Etheldreda's Fair in Ely (Audrey being a corruption of Etheldreda), and thus the word took its present meaning.

WORLD LITERATURE

1. In which language did Marcus Aurelius write?
2. A Maecenas is a munificent patron of literature or art. Of whom was the first Maecenas a patron?
3. In which novel did Raskolnikov play a leading part?
4. At whom did Emile Zola point the finger in *J'accuse*, and on whose behalf was he writing?
5. What is the *Book of Kells*, and where may it be seen?
6. Who wrote *Ghosts* and *Hedda Gabler*?
7. What did two famous Japanese novelists, Yasunari Kawabata and Yukio Mishima, have in common?
8. Which work of a world leader is reported to have sold over 800,000,000 copies?
9. How many stories are there in the *Decameron*, and who was the author?
10. In which classic work of literature would you find many common expressions such as the following:
    Mum's the word
    Wild goose chase
    Turn over a new leaf
    Every dog has its day
    Without a wink of sleep
    A finger in every pie
    Honesty's the best policy
    Birds of a feather flock together
    Earned with the sweat of my brows
    The proof of the pudding is in the eating

WORLD LITERATURE

1. Greek.
2. Horace and Virgil.
3. *Crime and Punishment*, by Fyodor Dostoevsky.
4. The French General Staff, Captain Alfred Dreyfus, who was convicted of treason.
5. It is a beautifully illuminated manuscript of the Latin Gospels, dating from the eighth century, and is generally regarded as the finest example of Celtic illumination. It is one of the treasures of Trinity College Library in Dublin.
6. Henrik Ibsen, Norwegian dramatist and poet.
7. They both committed suicide: Kawabata by gas, and Mishima by *seppuku*, commonly called *hara-kiri*, or belly-slitting, which is considered honourable suicide by the Japanese.
8. *Quotations from the Works of Mao Tse-tung*.
9. The *Decameron*, by Giovanni Boccaccio, is a collection of one hundred witty and occasionally licentious tales set against the sombre background of the Black Death.
10. *Don Quixote*, by Miguel de Cervantes, in the translation by Peter Motteux (1660–1718), an Anglo-French editor noted also for his translations of Rabelais. From *Don Quixote* we get the word 'quixotic', which means striving with lofty enthusiasm for visionary ideals.

ZEDS

1. What is the name of the lake in the Netherlands which is all that remains of the old Zuider Zee?
2. Name a leading symphony conductor who is a Parsee.
3. What is the name given to the American all-figure equivalent of the British Post Office's letters-and-figures postcode?
4. Who was the ravishing and bubble-headed creature that captured the young Duke of Dorset's heart during Eights Week at Oxford?
5. What and where is the Isle of Cloves?
6. Within ten degrees, can you give the Celsius equivalent of absolute zero?
7. 'Zounds' is a euphemism for which expression?
8. Who was married to the spokesman of the 'lost generation'?
9. What was the name of the Jewish sect who died heroically defending the mountain fortress of Masada against the Tenth Roman Legion in AD 73?
10. Where is the point on the earth at 0° latitude, 0° longitude, and zero altitude?

ZEDS

1. The Ijsselmeer, named after the River Ijssel which is its main feeder. It is now a fresh-water lake.
2. Zubin Mehta.
3. The ZIP Code. ZIP stands for Zone Improvement Program.
4. Zuleika Dobson, in Max Beerbohm's novel of that name.
5. Zanzibar, the island port of Tanzania. It supplies the bulk of the world demand for cloves.
6. $-273°C$.
7. God's wounds.
8. Zelda, the wife of F. Scott Fitzgerald.
9. The Zealots.
10. On the equator, in the Gulf of Guinea, off Ghana in West Africa.

Games of Logic *Pierre Berloquin* £1.95 ☐
Geometric Games *Pierre Berloquin* £1.95 ☐
Sunday Times Book of Brain Teasers
Victor Bryant and Ronald Postill
    Book 1   £1.95 ☐
    Book 2   £1.95 ☐

All these books are available at your local book-shop or newsagent, or can be ordered direct by post. Just tick the titles you want and fill in the form below.

Name ....

Address ....

....

....

Write to Unwin Cash Sales, PO Box 11, Falmouth, Cornwall TR10 9EN.

Please enclose remittance to the value of the cover price plus:

UK: 40p for the first book plus 18p for the second book, thereafter 13p for each additional book ordered, to a maximum charge of £1.49.

BFPO and EIRE: 40p for the first book plus 18p per copy for the next 7 books and thereafter 7p per book.

OVERSEAS: 60p for the first book plus 18p per copy for each additional book.

Unwin Paperbacks reserve the right to show new retail prices on covers, which may differ from those previously advertised in the text or elsewhere. Postage rates are also subject to revision.